Advance Praise

Texas women are incredible . . . and Mimi Webb Miller's life goes well beyond that to the near unbelievable. Bill Wright presents her biography in an up close and stunningly personal way through the lens of part friend, part journalist. Readers will experience a sense of being told stories from across the kitchen table mixed with the overwhelming deluge that comes with pure shock and awe interspersed with terror. Then there are the decades of famous (some infamous) names who never met each other, but whose common thread is Mimi Webb Miller. Overall, hers is a story of repeated survival and resiliency, and this is a striking portrayal of a Texas woman during the twentieth and twenty-first century that people need to read for themselves to believe.

—JESSICA BRANNON-WRANOSKY, PHD,
Distinguished Professor of Digital Humanities and History, East Texas A&M University

Bill Wright's book brings to life the story of someone who defies the norm and prioritizes living over life. Bill breathes in the air of Mimi's world of chance and risk, exhaling a strong will that shows the dignity of existence to the world at large.

—JAMES SURLS,
Artist

MIMI

BOOKS BY BILL WRIGHT

Celia Hill's Headin' West to a Remote Canyon Paradise, by Celia Hill, with Bill Wright and Marianne Wood. TCU Press.

Across the Border and Back: Music in the Big Bend, with Marcia Hatfield Daudistel. Texas A&M Press.

A Bridge from Darkness to Light: Thirteen Young Photographers Explore Their Afghanistan. TCU Press.

The Whole Damn Cheese: Maggie Smith, Border Legend. TCU Press.

Authentic Texas: People of the Big Bend, with Marcia Hatfield Daudistel. University of Texas Press.

Fort Phantom Hill: The Mysterious Ruins on the Clear Fork of the Brazos River. State House Press.

Oman: Land of Diversity. Fastback Creative Books.

The Texas Outback: Ranching on the Last Frontier, with June Redford Van Cleef.

People's Lives: A Photographic Celebration of the Human Spirit. University of Texas Press.

Portraits from the Desert: Bill Wright's Big Bend. University of Texas Press.

The Texas Kickapoo: Keepers of Tradition, with E. John Gesick Jr. University of Texas at El Paso Press.

Stray Tales of the Big Bend, with Elton Miles. Texas A&M Press.

The Tiguas: Pueblo Indians of Texas. University of Texas at El Paso Press.

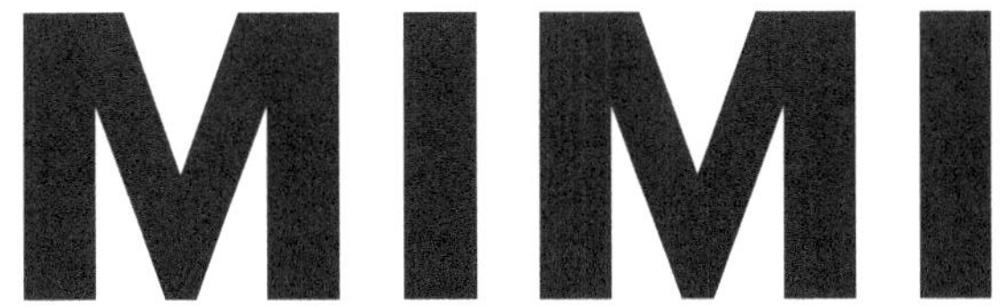

MIMI

The Perilous Journey of a Free-Spirited Texas Woman

BILL WRIGHT

TCU PRESS
FORT WORTH, TEXAS

Literary Non-fiction

Library of Congress Cataloging-in-Publication Data

Names: Wright, Bill, 1933– author writer of introduction writer of foreword | Carlson, Paul Howard writer of foreword
Title: Mimi : the perilous journey of a free-spirited Texas woman / Bill Wright.
Description: Fort Worth, Texas : TCU Press, [2026] | Includes bibliographical references.
Identifiers: LCCN 2025046120 (print) | LCCN 2025046121 (ebook) | ISBN 9780875659633 paperback | ISBN 9780875659640 ebook
Subjects: LCSH: Acosta, Pablo, –1987—Relations with women | Miller, Mimi Webb | Art museum curators—Texas—Houston—Biography | Ranchers—Texas—Brewster County—Biography | Casting directors—California—Biography | Hotelkeepers—Texas—Terlingua—Biography | LCGFT: Biographies
Classification: LCC F391.4.M55 W75 2026 (print) | LCC F391.4.M55 (ebook)
LC record available at https://lccn.loc.gov/2025046120
LC ebook record available at https://lccn.loc.gov/2025046121

TCU PRESS

Fort Worth, Texas 76129
www.tcupress.com

CONTENTS

FOREWORD

The Big Bend region of Texas, which includes the national park, is a wild, sometimes hostile, but always attractive country. Its harsh, high desert environment attracts tens of thousands of visitors each year. Most of the permanent residents form a tapestry of good people: some retired, others pursuing health benefits, some seeking alternative ways of life, others drawn by the expansive area's rugged, isolated beauty, and some, of course, for economic purposes.

J. O. Langford, for example, arrived in the Big Bend in 1909 for health reasons. He established a store and spa (of sorts) at Hot Springs along the Rio Grande at the mouth of Tornillo Creek. With his wife, Bessie, he soon came to love the wild, unknown country of the Texas Big Bend.

Homer Wilson, who also loved the region, came in the late 1920s to raise sheep and goats and to test the Big Bend's mining potential. He purchased over forty sections of land west and southwest of the beautiful Chisos Mountains and desperately struggled to keep it.

Langford and Wilson, with their families, were dynamic personalities of the Big Bend. Their experiences have been ably narrated by themselves and others.

Two other colorful Big Bend characters are Maggie Smith and Mimi Webb Miller. Author Bill Wright, who has published many books, covers Smith's magnetic story in his delightful work *The Whole Damn Cheese: Maggie Smith, Border Legend*. Smith, after her ranching husband died, took over Langford's Hot Springs store in 1942 when the Langford family left the Big Bend a second time. The border area was still untamed country, and Maggie, as tough as the rugged territory in which she lived, always carried a pistol in her skirt. After it became national park land, she remained in the Big Bend, operating stores at San Vincente, Boquillas in Mexico, Study Butte, a little-known town in Quebec, and Terlingua.

And now, in this endlessly fascinating book, Wright covers the life of Marian Elizabeth Webb Sullivan Miller, best known as Mimi Webb Miller. An unconventional artist from Wichita Falls and a free-spirited, pot-smoking resident of both sides of the Rio Grande in the Big Bend's Lajitas area, Mimi enjoys associations with popular celebrities, influential politicians, and major American artists, as well as an equal number of hard-working day laborers, local ne'er-do-wells, and Mexican drug-cartel types. She is a boldly independent soul, but also a charming and charismatic one.

Businessman, writer, photographer, and philanthropist Bill Wright has maintained a long association with Mimi Webb Miller. Bill maintains a second home in Fort Davis and is a life member of the Center for Big Bend Studies at Sul Ross State University in Alpine. And clearly, Wright knows the Big Bend—from its rich history to its most colorful characters. His book *Mimi: The Perilous Journey of a Free-Spirited Texas Woman*, like his book on Maggie Smith, *The Whole Damn Cheese*, represents thoughtful biography in colorful, absorbing tales.

Paul H. Carlson
Author, *Heaven's Harsh Tableland: A New History of the Llano Estacado*

PREFACE

I will admit to being nervous as the ancient Ford pickup truck bounced along the narrow road. We were returning from the Mexican village of San Carlos, twenty miles south of the safety of the Texas border beyond the Rio Grande. As the pickup swayed and jolted on the potholed gravel, I swung from side to side as the drunken driver, a Mexican rancher, Meño Proaño, put the pedal to the metal, giving me a nervous view of a forty- or fifty-foot drop-off on the driver's side and the unyielding rock walls of the canyon out of my window. I braced myself, preparing to grab the wheel in an emergency if he drifted off in a Corona-induced sleep. This was not my first trip to the Texas Big Bend. But it was the first time I met the fascinating Mimi Webb Miller: a true free spirit who had weathered many storms and disasters and made no promises, leaving none to break.

I want to tell you her amazing story.

So hold on to your hat; this one has it all: modern art, politics, the contemporary drug war, and Hollywood. At the center of everything is a Texas girl who broke free of her genteel upbringing for a life of romance, adventure, and even, at times, grave danger.

Mimi Webb Miller, the debutante niece of Texas Senator John Tower, began her career in the art world. Eventually, she found her natural home in the Big Bend of Texas thanks to another politician, Texas Governor Ann Richards.

Mimi continued working in fine art in remote Lajitas, Texas, until her relationship with the drug mafioso Pablo Acosta Villarreal—of Netflix's *Narcos: Mexico* fame—ended, and she had to leave the area for her safety. She spent thirty-six years in California working in the film casting business, always longing for her true home in the Big Bend, where she now resides full time.

Parts of this story derive from interviews I conducted with Mimi over the past few years. Some come from what I learned from newspaper clippings, articles, and books. Other parts come from my past interactions with her. After a brief introduction to the area Mimi calls home, I'll tell you how we met.

Introduction

As many of you know, the Big Bend region of Texas is a fascinating place. Eccentric twists and turns of the Rio Grande define much of the border between Mexico and this remote part of Texas. South of El Paso near the tiny collection of houses in Porvenir it begins an inverted hump like that of an upside-down buffalo's mane before following a more sensible route south to the Gulf of Mexico.

I am fascinated by the Great Chihuahuan Desert, surrounded by thirsty remnants of the last days of the glacial age with flat bolsons, born of eroded Cretaceous and Igneous deposits. White-tailed deer, mule deer, and elk roam their respective haunts, and over three hundred species of birds come and go according to the seasons. Ancient species of pine and fir trees dating back to the glacial age still survive in the upper reaches of the mountains. The flat lowlands, once covered by an inland sea, lack the moisture to nurture much growth above the waist except along a few bordering streams fueled by uncertain rains. These remnants of the Rocky Mountains have sheltered more than wildlife. Early explorers joined the Native Americans who managed a lifestyle compatible with this stark land.

My first exposure to this fascinating part of Texas came in 1951 during the Easter holidays when three of my high school friends and I decided to explore Big Bend National Park on our own. We spent four days in the park and climbed mountains, hiked trails through the narrow canyons, and slept on the ground in our bedrolls. Few tourists had discovered the vast desert wilderness, and we were virtually alone. Leaving to finish my final semester in high school, I knew I would be returning. The isolation and beauty had captured my soul, and I knew it would be a place I would visit always.

I married my lovely wife, Alice, at the beginning of my senior year at the University of Texas and returned to my home city of Abilene to begin a career in business. I also developed a greater love for photography, continuing with my favorite subject, the Big Bend area: the stars on the black nights, the clouds moving through blue skies, and the few people making the small communities of Terlingua and Lajitas alive in the middle of the desert. The proximity to Mexico continued to beckon me, and I often answered the call.

It was on such a bright and invigorating day in 1982 that Alice and I proposed to our guests that we boat across the Rio Grande into Mexico at the old Comanche crossings at Lajitas. Then we would travel overland about twenty miles to the small village of San Carlos. Our guide would be a woman I had yet to meet, Mimi Webb Miller.

CHAPTER 1

Meeting Mimi

I had never been across the Rio Grande to the village of San Carlos, Mexico, where we planned to see a cockfight, so I felt it necessary to get someone to lead our group. We also wanted to view and photograph the beautiful canyon that joined the river there. On advice from my friend at the Lajitas Hotel, I arranged the trip to San Carlos with Mimi Webb Miller over the telephone. Besides Alice and me, the group consisted of Phil and Jo Shultz from Santa Fe; Nancy Scanlan, a photographer

Bill and Group with Mimi. *Photograph by Bill Wright.*

from Austin; Marni Sandweiss, the curator of photographs at the Amon Carter Museum in Fort Worth; and her assistant, Charlotte Card. Phil was a naturalist and retired surgeon, and Jo was a former Army nurse whom he had met after the war while serving as a doctor with the Indian Health Service in Arizona.

Two anxious hours passed, and Mimi had not arrived at the time we had agreed. I was wondering if I had screwed up by planning a trip to Mexico with someone I didn't know. The temperature was crisp that morning, and dawn couldn't entirely break through the low overcast. Alice and I sat with our friends on the steps leading up to the front porch of the house we had rented for the week. Everyone was grousing, having been awakened at five in the morning for the ride across the river. We were ready for the promised breakfast at Mimi's ranch house on the road halfway to San Carlos.

We had been told that Mimi had recently graduated from Southern Methodist University with a degree in art history and that she was the niece of US Senator John Tower. Sounded steady and dependable. On the telephone, we had agreed on the price and the time, but here we were cold, hungry, and about ready to check off the whole adventure as a bad deal. Just as we were preparing to take our gear back inside, Mimi came walking up, unconcerned, and asked us to follow her to the river where a boatman was waiting to take us across to her waiting Suburban on the Mexican side. Anxiety somewhat subsided, and aggravation turned into exasperation.

"Did we misunderstand the time we were to meet?" I asked. "No," she responded, flashing a winning smile, "just had some difficulties getting started. Boatman was late . . . you know how it is in Mexico."

Mimi was assertive and confident. She had a beat-up look about her: bronzed skin and sun-bleached hair that was not from a fancy salon. She wore down-at-the-heels cowboy boots and Levi's and looked like she had spent her entire life on the border. Everyone began to relax, and I began to hope for the best.

The morning light was still tentative as we drove behind the old trading post to the Lajitas crossing. We locked the cars and started to the ferry that would take us to the Mexican village of Paso Lajitas, on the opposite bank, and Mimi's car. The "ferry" turned out to be a rowboat with a leaky bottom, and it was piloted by an uncertain navigator who spoke no English. The river looked ominous in the early light—dark brown waters swirling in mysterious eddies at the base of a slippery bank. I tried to reassure my guests. "I've been across here many times before. No sweat. You all load in, and I will come on the second trip." Somehow, though, I felt that everyone wanted me to go first, so I eased down the sloping bank and took my position in the rear of the boat. Alice was next, quietly carrying a longtime fear of rapid water as she sat beside me.

"The river isn't deep here," I told the group. "You can actually stand up and wade across." I was speaking to the breeze. All were eyeing the boatman and trying to convince themselves they would be safe in this rickety vessel with its Spanish-speaking captain with whom they could not communicate.

We crossed without incident, and the boatman returned for those who remained.

When we were all safely ashore on the Mexican bank, the group relaxed a little more as we loaded into Mimi's vehicle and started up the road toward her ranch house.

Paso Lajitas was beginning to stir, with people walking to the river. We drove through the town and started our climb out of the river valley and into the mountains to the south. Mimi would sometimes pull to the side of the primitive road to allow me to photograph. By now, the hungry troops were anxious to arrive at her house, with its promised ranch breakfast.

When we arrived at Mimi's Rancho El Milagro, breakfast was not ready, and the group began to grumble again. "We won't take but a moment," Mimi assured us with a smile. She proceeded to wake Meño, the Mexican rancher who was supposed to have had the coffee prepared. By now, everyone was delirious with hunger and fearful of what we might get when breakfast came.

Alice inquired about the facilities. Mimi, more accustomed to the unrefined nature of the Big Bend country than my citified wife, waved her outside, saying, "Just any bush." Alice was not charmed.

I wandered around photographing the rancher's children asleep in the bed, the goats sheltering near the house, the buildings—anything to pass the time while the eggs were cooking. Meño was fumbling around getting dressed. All the while, he and Mimi were hurling words at each other. Ours was one of Mimi's first tours, and she wanted things to move smoothly. Finally, she brought scrambled eggs, sausage, bacon, hot toast, and salsa. We ate as if it were our last meal and loaded up for San Carlos, wondering if the rest of the day would be as unpredictable as the morning.

After breakfast, we planned to drive to San Carlos to see a local celebration, photograph the cockfights, and listen to some authentic Mexican music. Then, we would hike up the beautiful canyon to the spring before returning to Lajitas.

Mimi drove her Suburban with the rest of the group while I rode in Meño's pickup. It was an experience. We careened around hairpin turns and bore down the grades at full throttle. I suspected he might have laced his eggs with tequila. The old pickup truck shook, and the brakes squealed as he stomped them approaching the curves. Occasionally, his foot would slide off the worn brake pedal and hit the accelerator. The truck would lurch forward toward the turn, and he would mash the brake pedal again. A giant rooster's dust tail plumed behind us, thrashing us every time we slowed. I was terrified. I only hoped that Mimi, well ahead of us, was driving more sanely.

Finally, we arrived in San Carlos. Our first stop was to visit Meño's mother, who owned a small shop. She was a charming and distinguished woman, and while she spoke only Spanish, her facial expressions and body language suggested that we were very welcome.

I photographed her store, the streets, and the church of San Carlos. Since the rooster fight was canceled, this trip turned out to be a dry run.

Mimi and her rancher companion took us to the beautiful canyon near the town where we picnicked and birdwatched. A wonderful experience. On the return trip, Meño drove the Suburban, leaving the pickup in town for repairs. Nancy, the photographer from Austin, sat between Meño and me in the front seat. There was no air conditioning. Alcoholic fumes blended with the soda crackers that Meño stuffed in his mouth and snowed us with as he spoke.

The unpaved and ungraded road wasn't fit for a sharecropper farm. Alice was terrified from looking out the window as Meño drove as fast as the old Suburban would go. Rocking and weaving, we imagined we were close to death through either asphyxiation or a sudden stop at the bottom of a gorge.

But Providence intervened. The engine began to wheeze and spit. After it hobbled into the yard at Rancho El Milagro, halfway to the border, Meño attempted emergency repairs. He removed the carburetor and accidentally dropped a bolt down the intake manifold. We abandoned the wounded vehicle and moved our gear to a nearby pickup truck. Nancy, Marni, Charlotte, and I opted for the open-air bed for this last leg of the trip. If the truck were to pitch over the side of a canyon, we could at least fling ourselves out of it at the last minute. We rattled down the mountain roads in the gathering dusk, and it seemed my companions were at the end of their ropes. Phil Schultz was tight-jawed and ready to throw the driver to the vultures. At the outset, he and Jo had been uncertain about traveling to Mexico under these conditions. I didn't know Marni and Charlotte very well before the trip. Marni had just taken the Amon Carter job, and she was fresh from the bright lights of the East Coast. This was her first real experience with the Texas Outback. They were beginning to wonder about me. Why did I invite them to this godforsaken country, and would they survive?

About two miles from the Lajitas crossing, the pickup blew one of its tires. We changed to the spare, and then we traveled about a mile and blew another tire. There were no other spares. We packed our camera gear, abandoned a smashed cooler box, and walked to the border. We had to rouse the boatman from his home because he had ceased operating for the day. My friends eagerly leaped into the boat they had been so concerned about before, and we finally landed on the Texas shore. Mimi was apologetic. I understood. She had depended on Meño, who had let her down. Alice thought this was a trip that she did not wish to repeat.

It was a year before I had the opportunity to reencounter Mimi. I was flying into the Big Bend to photograph, and I contacted her to see if she would drive me around. As I taxied up in my small plane, I killed the engine, gathered my gear, and walked toward her waiting at the airport. I hoped that experience with her would be better than the trip to San Carlos. Along the way, I began learning about her life.

CHAPTER 2

Getting Started: Mimi's Early Years

Mimi Webb Miller's grandfather, Walter Egbert Webb, a native of Bay City, Michigan, and a World War I veteran, came to Wichita Falls, Texas, in the 1930s. He worked his way south while helping build President Franklin D. Roosevelt's Great Plains Shelterbelt.[1]

The Shelterbelt project created windbreaks in the Great Plains states beginning in 1934 in response to the severe dust storms of the Dust Bowl, which resulted in significant soil erosion. The drought that caused the dust storms covered more than 75 percent of the country, according to a PBS American Experience article.[2]

Plains Farms Need Trees.
Public domain.

In 1936, Walter became director of the Shelterbelt program, which had its headquarters in Wichita Falls. He, his wife, and their eleven-year-old son, Bob, tired of moving from place to place, liked the small, friendly town, so he returned to Wichita Falls after World War II, making it home and establishing a landscape company.

Bob was in the fifth or sixth grade, and being a popular young man, he began making a lot of friends. He graduated from Wichita Falls High School in 1943 and decided to enlist in the US Army after one year of study at Texas A&M University. He deferred his education until the end of the war. He was nineteen years old.

Bob served in several areas of conflict, completing his service in the Philippines during the Japanese occupation and in Japan itself. With his newly acquired proficiency in the Japanese language, he was sent to manage the Kawana Hotel in Izu, a rest and recreation center for enlisted men operated by the United States Eighth Army Special Services Section.

Now that they were out of danger from the war, Bob married his high school girlfriend, Marian, affectionately called Muggy. She was the daughter of Grover and Marian Bullington, well-known and prosperous residents of Wichita Falls. Muggy joined Bob in Japan as he finished his service commitment before coming back home. When they returned to the United States and Wichita Falls, another significant change occurred in their lives: Muggy was pregnant.

Again, Bob's college education was temporarily sidetracked, but for a beautiful cause. He had just reenrolled at A&M when Marian Elizabeth, the child the Webbs had been eagerly anticipating, was born on April 2, 1949. Bob stood close by as Muggy cradled young Marian in their tiny apartment. It would be their home until Bob finished his degree in landscape architecture. Upon returning to Wichita Falls, Bob joined his father, Walter, in the landscape business, expanding their services

Young Wichitans Marry.
Courtesy of the Wichita County Archives.

PAGE 6 THURSDAY, MAY 16, 1946

Young Wichitans to Marry Here, Establish Residence in Japan

"Zushi, Japan" soon will be the address of two well-known young Wichitans whose engagement is revealed today and whose wedding will take place here June 1.

Mr. and Mrs. Grover C. Bullington of 1404 Buchanan Street are making formal announcement of the engagement of their daughter, Marian, to First Lt. Robert Clinton Webb, son of Mr. and Mrs. W. E. Webb, former Wichitans now making their home in Washington, D. C.

The young people are to be married in rites which have been scheduled for 5 o'clock Saturday afternoon, June 1, at the First Methodist Church. After a honeymoon to points of interest in the United States, the groom will return to duty in Japan where he soon will be joined by his bride. Lieutenant Webb, now on 45-day terminal business leave, is stationed in Japan in the capacity of special service officer in charge of a rest area at Zushi.

Miss Bullington, a graduate of Wichita Falls High School, now is a senior student at the Texas State College for Women in Denton where she is majoring in journalism. She also attended Hardin Junior College and the TSCW summer school at Saltillo, Mexico. In Wichita Falls, she has been active in social organizations, including the Junior Forum; and, in Denton, she has been a leader in TSCW campus groups. She is a member of Theta Sigma Phi, national honor fraternity for women in journalism; a member of the Mary Eleanor Brackenridge Literary Club; president of the Wichita County Club; a member of the TSCW rifle team; and a former member of the Student Finance Council. She has been serving as junior class editor of the college yearbook and society editor of the school paper, the Lass-O, at the same time working as a student assistant in the department of publicity for three years. Miss Bullington's other activities have included duties as social and vespers chairman for her dormitory and as a dormitory counselor

Wichitan Joins Husband in Japan

Pictured as they met aboard the USS Monterey which docked at Yokohama Aug. 10 carrying 839 dependents of army men are Lt. and Mrs. Robert C. Webb. Mrs. Webb, formerly Miss Marian Bullington, is a daughter of Mr. and Mrs. Grover C. Bullington, 1404 Buchanan. The Webbs, who were married in Wichita Falls June 1, enjoy the distinction of being the most recently married American service couple in Japan. They are living at Izu.

August 21, 1946 W.D.T.

Wichitan Joins Husband in Japan.
Courtesy of the Wichita County Archives.

Father and Son Are Landscape Architects. *Courtesy of the Wichita County Archives.*

Father and Son Are Landscape Architects

A father-son combination which grew out of the youth's love for Wichita Falls and the elder's years of experience in the profession, has resulted in one of the city's leading industries of its kind—The Webb Company, 3311 Taft, landscape architects.

Back in 1945, Robert C. (Bob) Webb, was in the Philippines with the United States troops and he began to think about his future.

His father, Walter E. Webb, had spent more than 15 years as a director of the U. S. Forestry and Park Service in the shelterbelt area in Wichita Falls and vicinity and many more years with the government service in the Plains country. In 1945 he was in Washington, D. C.

A letter was dispatched from the Philippines to his father in Washington, D. C., by young Webb who had been reared here and attended high school here. This letter urged that the senior Webb return to Wichita Falls and enter the landscaping business in anticipation of the son's return to the States and his favorite city and state, Wichita Falls, Texas.

Company Formed

So Webb Senior returned to Wichita Falls, and in July, 1949, the company was formed by the two Webbs. In July, 1950, following the son's graduation from Texas Agricultural and Mechanical College with a degree in landscaping architecture, the two became acting partners.

The Webb Company has been in its present location, 3311 Taft, since beginning operation. Since that time the firm has been active in the landscaping of the Hamilton-Martin Investment Company developments, having been responsible for the majority of the street tree planting of the investment company's new addition.

Crew Maintained

A crew of six to eight men is maintained by the company at all times, in addition to the office force and landscape specialists. Joseph Kelly, graduate of Texas Agricultural and Mechanical College with a degree in floriculture, is general manager.

Among the landscaping projects planted in Wichita Falls by The Webb Company are the Morningside Estates subdivision and the Stamford development in Faith Village. Design of the patio and its planting at the home of Jerry Vinson, 2209 Clarinda, was done by The Webbs, and the patio and interior garden at the home of Mrs. J. T. Harrall, 1301 Grant, was designed and executed by the company. Landscape contracting for Gordon West, 3208 Beech, also has been under the direction of The Webb Company.

Pumice is a form of volcanic lava. Other types disintegrate quickly and form soil of great fertility.

New Landscape Home. *Courtesy of the Wichita County Archives.*

NEW LANDSCAPE HOME—Above is the new, modern plant of the Webb Landscape Company that opened for business Saturday under the management of Walter and Bob Webb, a father and son team. The company is located at 2001 Tenth. The business grew out of Bob Webb's dream of owning such a company while he was serving his country during World War II in the South Pacific. His father is a well-known authority on trees in the plains area and worked for the U. S. Forest Service in Washington, D. C., before joining his son in this business venture.

Landscape Contractors – Ad. *Courtesy of the Wichita County Archives.*

to serve the needs of the community and the wealthy ranch owners surrounding the city.

At age twenty-seven, Bob was a handsome man, with sky-blue eyes. He enjoyed his work and soon developed an excellent reputation. Fluent in Spanish, Bob created a strong bond with his predominantly Hispanic employees. He passed his affection for them along to little Marian as the families grew up together. Bob chose to use Mexican workers because he admired their work ethic. They worked cheaply, but this meant he could hire more of them, and they could help him grow. Bob had a fleet of big trucks and, at one point, seventy workers.

Young Marian Elizabeth was a fast learner. She quickly caught on to the baby English that her mother cooed when she was nursing and learned the difference between "you" and "me." When mother Marian interrupted her feeding to answer a phone call or turn down the stove, instead of crying, baby Marian would call out, "Me! Me! Me!" She knew what she wanted and wanted it *now.* As she got older, her cry became more Mi-mi, which blended into Mimi. The name stuck. She called herself Mimi from then on. Mimi was a free spirit from birth.

Mimi was pampered by the Mexican workers who helped around the house and soon picked up the Spanish language, learning English and Spanish simultaneously.

Another girl, Melissa Louise, was born, and the family grew to four.

Wichita Falls, Texas, Sunday, July 29, 1951

LIKE MOTHER, LIKE DAUGHTER. Mrs. Grover C. Bullington, standing, will complete her 31st consecutive year in the nursery department at the First Methodist Church Sunday, Sept. 16. Her daughter, Marian, (Mrs. Robert C. Webb), seated, has worked in the nursery department since high school days and now is in charge of the toddler group of nursery youngsters. Not to be ignored is the third generation, Melissa and Mary Beth Webb. Melissa, 4-months-old, and Mary Beth, 2, are in the infant and toddler groups in the nursery and their mother and grandmother already have plans for their work in this department in a few more years. Mary Beth is holding the church school nursery publication, "My Book."

Like Mother, Like Daughter. *Courtesy of the Wichita County Archives.*

But the Webb family would have many weird disasters. On March 6, 1951, Muggy and her sister, Joza Lou, along with Mimi, were driving home when a large truck hauling gravel banged into Muggy's car and overturned, discharging its load through the open car windows and trapping the two women and Mimi. Bystanders rushed to the wreck and began clawing out the gravel that was smothering all of them. Muggy suffered a double fracture to her jaw and severe facial lacerations. Fortunately, the others' injuries were slight.

Muggy appeared to recover from the gravel injuries, but family members believed that the injuries caused an aneurysm.

About two and a half years later, another calamity occurred.

On a beautiful day, the Webb family and some friends decided to go to Lake Murray near Ardmore, Oklahoma, a couple hours' drive from Wichita Falls. While Bob and his friend launched a sailboat to polish their sailing skills, Muggy and the friend's wife loaded the girls onto a powerboat that was being fueled for the day's ride. The man driving the boat placed young Mimi and her three-year-old sister on top of the motor for better vision, and the women took the seats.

With the fueling completed, the boat was launched, and as the driver turned the key to start the craft, a spark ignited some spilled gasoline; the driver had failed to tighten the gas cap. An intense explosion threw the girls and the two women into the water. The flames quickly consumed the wooden boat, which sank immediately. The other woman grabbed the girls and got them onto the dock. All were burned: the two young girls severely, and Muggy and her friend less so. Mimi recalled that there was a guy who took charge of everything and that they had to remove her clothes. She remembers being quite embarrassed!

Bob and his friend, who witnessed the disaster from afar, quickly made their way to the injured women and girls, loading them into their automobiles and heading for the hospital in Ardmore.

On their arrival, the emergency staff wrapped the two children with white bandages from head to toe and rushed them into the main hospital for evaluation. Muggy's condition was serious enough that she joined her children in a hospital room. She was fortunate; she could leave the hospital after a few days, but Mimi and Melissa's burns had left deep scarring that inhibited their walking. The children were placed in the care of physical therapist Ruth Sherrill. Almost nine weeks later, they walked out of the hospital, able to return home. Today, the event remains vivid in their memories. They especially recall the generosity of the folks at the Methodist Church who would visit often and once brought a blue Jello rabbit.

Another tragedy struck seven months later, in 1954. Bob was again sailing on Lake Murray when news reached his boat that Muggy had fallen ill in Wichita Falls, and it appeared to be serious. Bob's best friend, a doctor named J. L. Jackson, had been called in. Bob rushed back home and went immediately to the hospital. Marian was

The Webb Sisters: Mimi, Robin, and Melissa. *Courtesy of Mimi Webb Miller.*

Mimi's Mother Succumbs.

Courtesy of the Wichita County Archives.

MRS. ROBERT C. WEBB

Mrs. Robert Webb

Native Wichitan Succumbs Here

4-20-54 RN

Mrs. Robert C. Webb, 28, lifelong resident of Wichita Falls and daughter of Mr. and Mrs. Grover C. Bullington, died unexpectedly in a Wichita Falls hospital Monday afternoon. 19

She is survived by her husband, owner of a landscaping firm, and three children, Marian Elizabeth, 5, Melissa Louise, 3, and an infant daughter, born Monday.

Mrs. Webb, the former Miss Marian Bullington, observed her 28th birthday Saturday, having been born April 17, 1926.

Funeral services will be held Tuesday at 4 p.m. from the First Methodist Church with the pastor, Dr. Alfred Freeman, officiating. Burial at Riverside Cemetery will be directed by Hampton-Vaughan-Merkle Funeral Home.

Mrs. Webb was educated in Wichita Falls schools and was graduated from Texas State College for Women in early 1948, shortly after she and her husband returned from Japan where he was a captain in the Army of occupation. They were married June 1, 1946.

The couple established residence here and she became active in the First Methodist Church and several groups including the Junior Standard Study Club and the TSCW Alumni Club of which she was an officer. The family home was at 3206 Speedway.

Twice in recent years Mrs. Webb had been seriously injured in accidents. She received a double fracture of the jaw and severe facial and head lacerations in a car-truck collision in Wichita Falls March 6, 1951. Her elder daughter had minor cuts and her sister, the former Joza Lou Bullington, received minor injuries.

unconscious. She was six months pregnant and had been feeling wobbly. There was nothing the doctors could do to help. She had suffered a second aneurysm.

Dr. Jackson turned to Bob and said, "Do you want to save the baby? It would be a gamble, but it would probably not have been harmed. It will be three months premature. Things could go wrong." Bob had to make a quick decision. He said, "Let's go for it!" And little Robin Ruth was delivered healthy. But Muggy didn't survive. She had celebrated her twenty-eighth birthday just two days earlier.

At five years old, Mimi lost her mother, and her father had three young children to care for.

"My dad taught me how to cook. We would make seven to nine pies at one time," Mimi told me. As her father said, "Why make just one?"

"Not only did he teach me to cook, but he felt it was my responsibility to take care of my younger sister and to help run the household."

But Bob clearly needed help. So, he interviewed numerous candidates to be the children's nurse, finally hiring Mrs. Gardner. "We called her

'Gaga,'" Mimi remembers. A Black woman, Wilma Blackman, applied to be the maid. As Mimi remembers, she had graduated from Harding College and was very smart. She became "the mother" of the three girls, teaching them the things that young girls should know before they went to school. Mimi told me, "We loved Wilma. We turned out okay after her love and attention." Still, even though she was very young, Mimi began to resent the woman her dad had employed to help. She thought she could handle everything.

Bob was well respected, and everyone sympathized with his needs and wanted to help. Others who pitched in from time to time included a doctor's family that lived across the street: Dr. Julian and Dodo Acker. They had six kids. The mother, realizing the family was having a rough time, served as a "backup" mom despite having her hands full.

Another friend who helped occasionally was Anne Smith Jeffus, a retired bookkeeper. "She gave me a lot of attention, which I appreciated," Mimi said.

The girls' grandparents were also there to lend a hand. On Saturdays, Mimi would go to her mother's parents' home and get her hair washed and ready for Sunday school—at the Methodist Church where her mother had taught in the nursery—the next day. Then, after Sunday school, she would go to Grandmother Webb's. She had chickens to play with.

"My grandfather had facial cancer," Mimi told me. "We called him 'Johnny Appleseed' because he built and planted a lot of the Shelterbelt. He wore a Kotex pad on his face and a handkerchief that made him look like a bandit." The girls adored their grandfather because he always shared milkshakes with them. Eventually, he had surgery to reconstruct his face, but unfortunately, he died two weeks later from a heart attack.

Mimi's Grandfather Dies.
Courtesy of the Wichita County Archives.

Pioneer Landscape Architect Dies

JUN 27 1962

One of Wichita Falls leading landscape architects and a long-time tree expert in the Plains country, Walter E. Webb, 65, died Tuesday night following an illness of several months at his home at 4610 Wyoming.

A resident of Wichita Falls for 25 years, Webb was a partner with his son, Robert C. (Bob) Webb, in the Webb Landscape Co. formed here in January, 1951. He was widely known for his work as director of the Shelterbelt program of the forestry division of the U.S. Department of Agriculture throughout the Plains states in the 1930s.

A native of Bay City, Mich., Webb was born Sept. 15, 1896, and was graduated from Michigan State University at Ann Arbor in 1931 after he had served as an infantry lieutenant during World War I.

City Forester

He served as city forester for the City of Detroit, Mich., director of parks at Mitchell, S.D. and in 1936 became director of the Shelterbelt program with headquarters in Wichita Falls.

In 1943 he worked with the Guagele rubber plant in California and then worked with the Navy Hydrographic Office in Washington, D.C., returning to Wichita Falls after World War II. He formed the Webb Landscape Co. here and remained active in the business until his retirement last September.

Episcopalian

He was a member of All Saints Episcopal Church, where he was a vestryman. He was a member of Wichita Falls Rotary Club, the chamber of commerce and was a Mason. He was a member of the American Society of Foresters, the American Association of Nurserymen and the Texas Association of Nurserymen.

Survivors include his wife, Mrs. Irene Clay Webb, whom he married in 1924; his son, Robert Webb of 3206 Speedway; a daughter, Mrs. Nancy Silliman of Los Altos, Calif.; a brother, Frank Webb of Detroit; a sister, Mrs. Julia Candler of DeLand, Fla.; and five grandchildren.

WALTER E. WEBB

Services Set

Funeral services will be held at 2:30 p.m. Thursday in All Saints Episcopal Church. Officiating will be Rev. Francis W. Fowler, rector.

Burial will be in Riverside Cemetery under direction of Hampton - Vaughan Funeral Home.

Memorials may be made to the Walter E. Webb Memorial Fund of All Saints Episcopal.

Pallbearers are Earl Staten, John W. Wilson, G. C. Bullington Jr., Joe Sherrill Jr., Dr. J. L. Jackson, James Irl Montgomery and Dr. Jerry Hathorn.

Honorary pallbearers include Joe Sherrill, Dick Long, Juan Rangel, F. P. McDougal, John Humphrey, Grover Bullington, Sen. John Tower, J. W. Keys, Col. S. M. Pool, Joe Hancock and L. W. Fritz.

Mimi's grandmother Irene was no slouch. "She was really special," Mimi would recall. She taught herself airplane mechanics and then taught this course to Sheppard Air Force Base students. In addition, she took care of the landscaping office. That was a challenge due to the lack of employees who spoke both Spanish and English. Despite all these responsibilities, Mimi's grandmother still found time to help with the children.

But the children needed a full-time mother, and Bob knew who he was going to consider marrying: the excellent therapist who had taught the two older girls to walk again after the boat explosion that turned their legs stiff with painful scar tissue. It was perfect, he felt: the children were fond of the woman who had returned their mobility.

He married Ruth Sherrill in December 1955. All this disturbed six-year-old Mimi. When her dad started dating, Mimi told me, she was offended. "I can set the table; I can feed the baby. I don't know why we need someone else." She had had enough of Ruth's loving but strict care and felt more adult than she was. She did not think she needed a new mom.

Moreover, Mimi thought that her stepmother disliked her. She seemed to get in trouble constantly and get more than her share of punishment.

Hearing Mimi describe the problems, I sensed that the girls were well-loved, but they were not used to strict control. However, school was just ahead for Mimi, and she was ready to keep learning about the world around her.

Growing up, Mimi had a canine companion at home, a black Lab named Cindy. "My dad loved her," she told me. "He would take her out hunting with us. My sister and I would do most of the work of caring for her. We would take the bird from her mouth when Daddy shot a bird." But her dad was afraid of birds. She explained: "When he was small, Daddy spent some time on his grandparents' farm. He would see them wringing a bird's neck, and it must have affected him. Even when a sparrow got caught in the chimney, my dad would go to the powder room to sit until others caught the bird."

Once time, Cindy stole a whole ham from the dinner table. Mimi recalled that the dog ran off with it, and everyone got quiet. "I mean, we never saw anything that atrocious. It was like the greatest crime in the family! Cindy was spanked, and we were able to cut off the outside of the ham and eat the inside for dinner. When Cindy died, my father just cried and cried. I'd never really seen my dad sob like that before."

Bob introduced the children to agriculture as a necessity. He and their grandfather were the only landscape people in Wichita Falls, with a large nursery and tree lot. So, not only did the girls help care for the

Cucumber Harvest Begins In Wichita's Irrigated Valley

JUNE 26, 1966

TOMATO GREENHOUSE — The skelton of a one-half acre of greenhouse on the Bill West farm in the Wichita Irrigated Valley is shown stretched out before it was covered with plastic. Bill West and Bob Webb are planning to set their plants about Aug. 15 and hope to have vine ripe, hot house tomatoes coming off about Oct. 15 of this fall. Use of greehouses for tomato producation is becoming a rapidly growing industry in Texas as growers aim for the high winter tomato market. (Staff Photo)

PICKLE FIELD—John Ferguson, left, farm manager for Bill West's 40 acres of cucumbers being grown in the Wichita Irrigated Valley, is pictured showing Wichita County Agent B. T. Haws growth the plants had made without a single rainfall since planting. However, after the photograph was made the farm received an inch of rainfall. The cucumbers are being grown under contract to Dalton's Best Made Foods in Fort Worth. (Staff Photo)

By JOE BROWN

The first real opportunity to test the Wichita Irrigated Valley's ability to produce commercial crops of vegetables is being tried this summer on a 50-acre farm between Wichita Falls and Iowa Park.

Bill West, owner of West Optical Co., is owner of the farm and Bob Webb of Webb Landscaping Co., is managing the 38 acres of irrigated cucumbers being grown.

In addition, they are erecting 30,000 square feet of greenhouse for tomatoes on the farm, known as Unit. 89, Wichita Valley Farms.

Intensive farming is the story of commercial vegetable production and this is the description for West's initial start in the vegetable growing business. Farm manager John Ferguson said he has never seen soil worked like they did on the approximately 40 acres of cucumber land.

It was chiseled, bladed and plowed 11 times before being seeded to cucumbers, a crop being grown under contract to Dalton's Best Maid Foods of Fort Worth for pickles.

Before the cucumber seeds were sown, West and Webb applied 150 pounds of 16-16-16 per acre. After the plants were up they side dressed twice with 25 pounds of actual nitrogen in the form of urea. Throughout harvesting, which began Friday, more applications of nitrogen will be applied about every third picking.

Harvest is expected to last eight to 10 weeks and possibly up to 13 weeks. Each plant will be stripped every other day by the labor crews.

Ferguson said the cucumbers were sown in rows at the rate of 40,000 plants per acre and each plant is expected to produce at least one and one - half pounds of cucumbers.

Going into detail, Ferguson said the rows are 40 inches apart with the plants being laid up and down the rows so machinery can move easily through the fields.

Two aerial sprayings already have been completed and ground spray rigs will continue throughout the harvest.

But it is the moisture that makes a cucumber and the field has really soaked up the irrigation water that has been applied by syphon out of the lateral ditches. The fields are watered at least once a week and more often when needed, said Ferguson.

In the photograph that accompanies this story, the plants had not received a single shower following planting, but the farm caught a one - inch rain a bit later. Harvesting began on mature plants grown with only one inch of rainfall.

Webb explained this surely should prove the value of the irrigated valley as a potential vegetable source. He also explained Dalton's wanted to contract 300 acres in this area of the state rather than the few it now has signed up.

Last year's attempts at commercial cucumber productio[n] found difficulty in getting off th[e] ground due to the lack of stoo[p] labor to harvest the crop regularly.

West made a labor contra[ct] with Washington High School foo[t]ball coach Ervin Garnett a[nd] Connie McCallen. They agreed [to] furnish the youths to pick the [38] acres of cucumbers. Dalton's [ad]vises it takes about one and o[ne] half to two harvesters per ac[re] of cucumbers in full producti[on].

This means the 38 acres [of] pickles will provide summer j[obs] for about 70 to 80 youths [in] Wichita Falls and Iowa Pa[rk]. There will also be a number [of] adults working in the fields si[nce] the wages are good.

Bob and the Cucumber Harvest. *Courtesy of the Wichita County Archives.*

flowers and bushes around the house, but they also assisted in larger projects.

One of Bob's projects was supplying cucumbers for the Best Maid pickle company in Fort Worth. He hired a Black football team to harvest the cucumbers. Once, Bob saw the coach spanking one of the boys, and he called it off. The girls took over harvesting the cucumbers.

People still contact Mimi about the cucumber operation. She told me that she had recently sent somebody some information about Best Maid.

On Friday afternoons, the Mexican men would bring tortillas, and Bob would provide beer. Mimi remembers being served as many five-cent Cokes as she wanted, courtesy of the employees.

Mimi described her typical summers. "We would go to Corpus Christi. My stepmom, Ruth, would sleep, and my dad would take us all out to the end of a pier so we could catch crappie and come back and cook it. My dad was just great with us. We did that for years." They made lots of art including seashell crafts.

Mimi (Maribeth Webb) and High School Group. *Courtesy of the Wichita County Archives.*

SUPPLIES AT HAND — Maribeth (left) and Sherri Webb are shown with only a few containers and trays full of plants and flowers which they will dry. Sherri is looking at a tiger lily she has in a cup.

Maribeth (Mimi) with sister, Sherri. *Courtesy of the Wichita County Archives.*

Mimi began school at Ben Franklin Elementary, near the Webbs' home. The small town of Wichita Falls had a family-like mentality among its population, and she knew most of the children in her classes. She was a good student with A's in all her subjects and was active outdoors during recess. She played Red Rover at home.

Mimi's first boyfriend, Ken Hines, lived across the street and shared her birthday, though he was a year older. They met in the first grade. Since she didn't have brothers, the close association with a neighbor boy in school was a new experience. They laughed about different things, wore different clothes, drew different pictures in art class, and played different games at recess. Mimi grew increasingly interested while mulling the lectures she endured about boys from her stepmother. She noticed the boys seemed to keep to themselves and not mingle with the girls.

Most of all, Mimi wondered about the difference in bathroom facilities. Her parents did not talk about sex to the children!

Mimi's first real boyfriend came along in the ninth grade. She recalled, "His name was Lannis. He was fourteen. He threw papers in the morning, and we invented a strategy. I would get up and tell my family, 'I'm gonna bicycle every morning.'" Mimi described it like this: "I'd bicycle to the alley, and he'd come up and meet me, and we f*****d in the Playhouse. It was such good sex! I was like, 'Oh wow, this is great!'"

During her high school years, Mimi, who also went by Maribeth, was very popular. She was elected president of the Girls Club during her senior year. She was a Junior Forum and Carousel Club debutante. She was a member of the National Honor Society. And she enjoyed the attention she got from young men.

"My senior year in high school, I fell for a guy from the wrong side of the tracks," Mimi told me. He lived in an apartment by himself. His name was Ronnie Phillips. She didn't know anybody else who lived in an apartment as a teenager. "He was good to me," she said. "And we fell in love."

Mimi knew she would go away for college and that their relationship would not last. He was a year or two older, and her parents didn't like that, either. They didn't want her to take him to the deb dance, but he was the only guy she knew well, so she did. Not surprisingly, Ronnie felt out of place, since his working-class background set him apart from the wealth and polish of the debutante crowd. There wasn't any problem, though. Mimi made it home on time from the dance. Mimi noted, "In no sense did this relationship solely involve sex because I had already screwed Lannis when I was fourteen. Ronnie had many problems and committed suicide not too long ago."

The *Wichita Falls Times* reported that Mimi received recognition for "adaptability" in her volunteer work as a "Pink Darling" at the Wichita

Hospital Cites Top Pink Darling

The Wichita General Hospital announced the name of the Pink Darling selected as the most outstanding member for the year.

Miss Judy Waggoner, daughter of Mr. and Mrs. T. J. Waggoner Jr. of 2207 Miramar, received the Key Pink Darling award at the spring banquet Wednesday evening in the Western Room of the Country House.

Other nominees for the honor were Miss Wanda Wood, daughter of Rev. and Mrs. Wilson Wood, and Miss Debby Perkins

Mimi Webb received recognition for adaptability and Misses Monte Montgomery, Jacqueline Owen, and Mary Jo Robinson for their sense of humor.

Cooperativeness awards were given to Misses Jan Hamm, Nancy Hays, Janice Albert, and Brenda Burns.

Mrs. Robert Webb, president-elect of the Texas Association of Hospital Auxiliaries, was a special guest at the banquet as were hospital administrator Frank Schueller and Mrs. Schueller.

Hospital Cites Top Pink Darling. *Courtesy of the Wichita County Archives.*

Maribeth (Mimi) Webb – Carousel. *Courtesy of the Wichita County Archives.*

General Hospital. Her stepmother was president-elect of the Texas Association of Hospital Auxiliaries that year. The newspaper also captured a photo of Mimi at a Carousel Club debutante party.

CHAPTER 3

College and First Marriage

When Mimi was in her last semester of high school, in 1967, she told me, she wanted to get out of Wichita Falls. She wanted to see what the world was like away from the clutches of her stepmother, who tried to manage her every step. "In all the pictures of me you look at, I was crying because my mom had hammered me to get ready for college. She was really mean to me, so I put more effort into studying," Mimi recalled. "I loved to read.

"I didn't want her at any of the dances. My dad was very strict when he went with me to one. I think all the boys paid attention there because of him, and I didn't have much fun.

"I thought my high SAT score—1450—would get me into almost any school. Everyone knew my parents wanted me to go to Mills College in Oakland, California. All my parents' friends knew. The neighbors knew. I just had to deal with it." Mimi had been accepted to Hollins and Sweet Briar, both women's colleges in Virginia, but she thought they were too fancy. In the end, she gave in and enrolled at Mills, partly because her stepmother had gone there and wanted her to, and partly because California felt so much farther away than Virginia—new people, new experiences. Mills was an all-girls school, but students often dated boys from Stanford and Oakland. Mimi was all for that!

Mimi and her dad had a good visit during the long trip to California that made her feel like an adult. Soon after signing in at the college and getting settled in her dorm room, Mimi attended a "mixer." These events allowed Mills students to get acquainted with male students from other local universities.

Mimi was immediately attracted to Alan Sullivan, a tall, handsome student from Henderson, Nevada. He had a BS degree and a master's from Stanford University and was in his final year of a second master's degree in computer engineering. And he had a beautiful, fast-looking car.

Mimi's first year at college instantly fell into place. She had visions of sunbathing on the beach, skiing the hills of Squaw Valley, and partying with this luscious man in the many lively bars and restaurants that dotted the California scene. They met and immediately jelled. It was off to the races for Mimi.

"Mills didn't care where I went when I signed out," Mimi pointed out. "As fate would have it, Alan had an apartment at Stanford in Palo Alto, and I spent a lot of time there with him. Every time my father would call my room at Mills, someone would cover for me." She would be at Alan's apartment or off with him to a party or the beach.

Early in Mimi's time at Mills, Senator John Tower came to give a talk to the students at nearby Berkeley University. Tower was the first Republican elected to the Senate from Texas since Reconstruction. And he was Mimi's uncle by marriage to Joza Lou (Honey) Bullington, her mother's sister. The Towers lived in the same neighborhood as the Webbs when he was teaching political science at Midwestern University in Wichita Falls, and the families would often get together for dinner and dominoes. Mimi liked the Towers. And they gave her social capital.

She told me that one of the big shocks to her when Senator Tower first came to Berkeley was when a liberal student shouted to bring him a "soap box" to stand on. Embarrassing! It was not so much because the senator was short, just five feet six inches, but the students implied they were getting only soap in the lecture. But Mimi was glad he'd been given the chance to address the students despite all the negativity. As a conservative Republican, he was unusual on this liberal college campus, but he was a good speaker who perhaps changed some people's minds about world affairs.

Another time Tower visited, he brought along screen actor James Drury. They all went to a fancy restaurant in San Francisco. Mimi was eating up the attention she received while in the company of a well-known senator and a famous TV actor. She enjoyed playing the part of an experienced lady. She may have forgotten to breathe in such a star-saturated atmosphere.

At one point, the cigarette Mimi was smoking went out. She reached for her lighter, but Drury pushed away her hand. "Let a man do it," he said. Next, she remembered him saying, "I think I'll have a grasshopper." Mimi added, "I think I'll have an old-fashioned."

"You know I am not a drinker. I just thought I'd try my uncle," Mimi told me. "I was taller than he, but he carried me to a taxi. I had sprained my ankle skiing at Squaw Valley. I wore a nice suit, a ridiculous vinyl hat, and a crutch. I thought I was so cool. This was another lesson learned that had nothing to do with Mills College."

All this association with famous men got Mimi a lot of publicity. Later, Oprah Winfrey's *O Magazine* referred to Mimi as "Texas Royalty"![1]

"I didn't go home very often, maybe once," she told me.

She finished up the second semester with passing grades even though there were many skips and late assignments. It was not because she couldn't do the work. It was just tricky when there were so many things to do with Alan. The proximity to such enticing locations as San Francisco did not sync well with the bright-eyed freshman's introduction to a scholar's world.

And Mimi continued to dodge her father's telephone calls. She said that when he finally reached her that winter, he was completely freaked out. With the spring semester ending, she began to dread going home even for the summer. She saw a way out by getting married. "Well, I'm gonna marry the guy!" she told her dad. "It was just like that. I'm not sure I wanted to say it like that, but I did." It wasn't long before her strategy paid off when she and Alan agreed to marry.

So now she was counting the days until she was wed to the enticing Alan Sullivan. She headed back to Wichita Falls to prepare for the wedding, only to find that Ruth, her stepmother, had planned the whole thing! She chose the colors and okayed who was in the wedding party. Ruth enjoyed planning nuptials for even a rebellious stepdaughter. There would be weeks of parties, dresses to buy, locations for a honeymoon to consider, and invitations to extend. Of course, there would be visits by the charming young man, who quickly gained the acceptance and delight of the family.

"I married him in the Methodist Church in Wichita Falls," Mimi said. "As I came down the aisle, I was a little shaken. I whispered to my father, I think I made a mistake. Dad went white. He probably thought, 'What the

Mrs. Thomas Alan Sullivan (Mimi). *Courtesy of the Wichita County Archives.*

Sullivan-Webb Vows Are Read In Methodist Church

→ Miss Marian Elizabeth Webb became the bride of Thomas Alan Sullivan of Dallas Friday evening in a ceremony performed at the First United Methodist Church. The Rev. Joe Z. Tower of Atlanta, Tex., retired minister, officiated.

The altar held urns filled with gladioli, mums and pompons.

Tommy Irvin was organist.

The bride attended Mills College in Oakland, Calif., and will be a student at Texas Woman's University in the fall. She is the daughter of Mr. and Mrs. Robert Clinton Webb, 3206 Speedway.

Sullivan was all-conference in football at Claremont Men's College in Claremont, Calif., where he received the B. S. degree. He is the son of Mr. and Mrs. Thomas A. Sullivan of Boulder City, Nev.

The bride chose a gown of light ivory fashioned of silk organza over taffeta and featuring an Empire bodice of Chantilly lace overlay, reembroidered with crystal beads and tiny seed pearls. Wide bands of the lace were repeated on the A-line skirt.

Her chapel train was attached at the shoulders and made with a Dior bow in center back. Her veil was of Brussels princess lace gathered on a circlet of organza. She carried a cascade of gladioli blossoms and stephanotis. Her father gave her in marriage.

The bride's sisters were her attendants. Miss Melissa Webb was maid of honor; Misses Robin Webb and Sherri Webb were bridesmaids. They were dressed identically in formal gowns of apricot Saki with Empire waists and A-line skirts. Their headdresses were apricot Dior bows and each carried a nosegay of apricot carnations and pompon mums.

Mark Sullivan of Las Cruces, N.M., brother of the bridegroom, was best man. Groomsmen and ushers were Mike Spiller and George Spires.

The bride's parents hosted the reception held at the Wichita Falls Country Club following the ceremony.

Tables were covered with white satin and were centered with floral arrangements. The reception table held a brass container filled with apricot carnations, pompon mums and flanked by candles.

Assistants were Mrs. John G. Tower, Mrs. J. W. Sherrill Jr., and Mrs. G. C. Bullington Jr., aunts of the bride; also, Misses Sally Parker of Hot Springs, Ark., Susan Boer of Red Bluff, Calif., Janey Shappell, Diane Montgomery, Cinda Smith, Cherie Wilson, Ruth Harr and Debby Perkins. Miss Mackie Ann Sne[illegible] and Fai[illegible] Marian [illegible] Bullingt[illegible] bags.

After pus Chri in Dall employe siness M

After a wedding trip to Corpus Christi, the couple will live in Dallas where Sullivan is employed by International Business Machines.

The bride was graduated from Wichita Falls High School where she was a member of National Honor Society, gym leaders and president of Girls Club. She was a Junior Forum and Carousel Club deb.

Her husband was graduated from Boulder City High School in 1963 and received a second B. S. degree and master's degree from Stanford University in Palo Alto, Calif. He is a member of the Texas National Guard.

The bridegroom's parents were hosts for the rehearsal party at the Country Club Thursday evening. The table was decorated with gladioli, apricot carnations and yellow pompons.

Out of town guests other than those in the houseparty were Mr. and Mrs. Willis S. Moss of Hobbs, N.M., Miss Jill Kendell of Norman, Okla., and Nick and Chris Rasmussen of Palo Alto, Calif.

Sullivan–Webb Vows. *Courtesy of the Wichita County Archives.*

hell! We've got 600 guests and an expensive cake,' but his eyes never faltered. He continued marching down the aisle with Mimi on his arm, determined to get the damn thing done."

After the rites were read, the ring was presented. The formal words spoken—"I pronounce you man and wife"— I imagine that Bob began to breathe again. The attractive couple walked out of the church over strewn flowers, to start their new life together.

The honeymoon was matter-of-fact. It did not involve the glamor of the Bahamas, the intrigue of India, or the exotic Hawaiian Islands. It was a week of bay fishing in Corpus Christi, followed by a move to Dallas, where Alan had secured a job with IBM as a systems engineer.

Alan had planned to accept an IBM job in Australia. But when Bob learned of this, he was outraged. "You just can't take my nineteen-year-old daughter off to some remote spot on the other side of the world!" he lashed out.

So they moved to Dallas instead. They bought a duplex in Highland Park, where Mimi would walk their dog along Turtle Creek while waiting for Alan to get off work. She met all sorts of people, including professional golfer Lee Trevino.

Alan quickly joined the National Guard, an organization he initially enjoyed. He was a quick learner and very good at what he was assigned. He even won an award for being the best in his class. But the Guard began taking up much of his time. The base he was assigned to was in Breckenridge, Texas, some distance from Dallas, and he was required to be out of town three weekends a month for activities and training. Mimi began to feel lonely, severed from her usual diet of intense socialization.

Meanwhile, "I had been given a lot of stocks by my grandfather," Mimi said. "I went into Merrill Lynch and asked them to help me with them. They asked me how I wanted them listed, and I told them I wanted them in both our names. That was how naive I was. I thought it would be nice, and Mom would think it was wonderful, and it wouldn't make any difference. So, I put all my stocks in the bank and forgot about it. Times were good then."

But Mimi was getting bored. Dallas was not as exciting as her life at Mills: downhill skiing, staying in the Mills College house at the lake, or lounging on the beach. She had far too much energy to burn in an empty house. It was also perilously near her stepmother in Wichita Falls who continued to give her "advice."

So, while Alan pursued his new career with IBM, Mimi set out to continue hers. She realized her desire to be a ceramic artist by attending Southern Methodist University in Dallas.

After three years at SMU, Mimi graduated in December 1971, earning a BFA in ceramics after adding art history. She thought the additional degree would give her a better chance for employment.

While taking courses, Mimi worked part-time at the Chapman Kelley Gallery and began learning a lot about the retail end of the art business. "The first piece of art I ever bought was from Chapman Kelley," Mimi told me. "I bought it right after I graduated from SMU. I paid $3,000 for it. I still have it in my house. Kelley had a big gallery, and he understood me. He would sit down with me and tell stories about artists, Robert Motherwell and others.

"I still have a John Alexander painting I got then, and it's worth much more today. John was a graduate student at SMU when I was there. He showed me a piece of his work that he later sold to Bill Clements, a Texas governor."

While Mimi was getting into the business end of art, Alan enjoyed his job at IBM. Mimi's family thought that Alan was a first-class guy and that he cared a lot about them. It seemed about as perfect a match as you could imagine, except for an apparent personality clash. Mimi was a free spirit if there was ever such a thing. Alan, on the other hand, seemed to be very organized; he planned his life step by step. It began to dawn on Mimi that they weren't meant for each other. Play days seemed to be over, and the reality of life had begun.

Alan was also losing interest in the National Guard. Sensing something was wrong, Mimi got him into counseling, which he quit after a few sessions. She called the doctor, who revealed that evidently, during his National Guard summer camp, Alan had some experience that affected him deeply. He began to resent his life in the United States and wanted to make a significant move.

It wasn't long before Alan quit the Guard.

Mimi composed her thoughts. "I wanted to run," she said. "I told the marriage therapist I'm just tired of coming here by myself. I thought he may have had a relationship with someone in the National Guard, and that was what was going on. I just knew we weren't meant for each other."

I asked Mimi why she wanted to get divorced from such a good guy as Alan! She mused about it, and I could tell it was complicated, as most divorces are.

As Alan became more distant, even at home, Mimi began socializing with her next-door neighbor, Barbara. While out with Barbara, Mimi met Dick Miller at a bar on Greenville Avenue. Dick was living with a woman, "the singer, Cass Elliot," Mimi told me. "He split with Cass and started going with me. I had started seeing other guys because I couldn't fight the loneliness of Alan being away so much. When he was home, I still felt a remoteness."

Mimi told me about the night that everything changed. She and Dick had decided to spend a night together at a Holiday Inn, and Dick's former girlfriend found out about it. She called Alan who immediately came to the hotel. Mimi got Dick out of there in time but had only enough time to hide in a tiny closet. She waited, holed up in the room. It was awful, and soon things got worse. When Alan arrived, he gave Mimi a sock in the face, resulting in a black eye and a chipped tooth. She could barely walk. That ended the five-year marriage. Mimi divorced Alan by mail. "I never showed up at the courthouse," she said.

Unfortunately, when she had put the stocks she inherited from her family with Merrill Lynch, she put them in both her and Alan's names according to the custom of the time and believing it would improve their relationship. "Brainwashed," she said. So she lost a large amount of money as well as the home the couple had purchased in Highland Park.

Mimi wanted to put some space between herself and Alan, so she and Dick packed up and moved to Houston, where he continued his job as a used-car salesman with a Volkswagen dealership on the Southwest Freeway. There, they began a new life together.

CHAPTER 4

Houston

In Houston, Mimi wanted to attend Rice University to secure a master's degree in art history. But Rice did not offer such a degree, so she focused on getting a job. "I applied to be a taxi driver," she told me. "I was happy to do anything. But the taxi service rejected me as being 'overqualified.' I went to work for the securities brokerage firm Eastman Dillon, later Blyth Eastman Dillon."

Mimi loved her life in Houston—it was not as stilted as Dallas. She enjoyed all the artists she met and learned a great deal from them. She told me that she began to sell some of their work and prepare them for shipping.

"It was easy to make friends. I made a great friend of Houston socialite Pam Sakowitz. I connected with several wealthy collectors who used me as an art consultant. I listened to their hilarious 'war stories.'"

After working for Blyth Eastman Dillon, Mimi went to work for another brokerage firm, EF Hutton. Although they wouldn't let her become a broker, she went up the ladder very quickly and soon moved to institutional sales, calling on every famous art group anyone could imagine: the Ford Foundation, the Metropolitan Museum of Art, and others. Mimi loved working there.

"The manager at Hutton was Mr. Michael T. Judd, an Englishman," she recalled. "I wound up working for him in the morning and working for his art collector wife, Ann, in the afternoons."

Finally, after being together for three or four years, Dick and twenty-six-year-old Mimi decided to get married. They wed in Michael and Ann's home. After the service, they went outdoors and drank champagne out of mason jars. They had a great time. Mimi told me, "My dad didn't come. I hadn't talked to him for like three years; it was just too much for him." It bothered him that Dick was much older than Mimi.

"After a while, I left Hutton and started a consulting business. I went in wholly with large sculpture. I could drive a big truck, put together shows, and travel them. I began meeting many of the leading names in art, including Claes Oldenburg."

At that time, Mimi received another big round of money from her grandparents. She believed it could serve no better purpose than bringing large sculpture, a growing genre of art, to Houston. The oil boom of the 1970s created an increase in ultra-rich arts patrons. So the time was right.

Wichitan organizes sculpture exhibit

An exhibition of monumental sculpture, opening Saturday in Houston, has been organized by former Wichitan Mimi Webb-Miller and Kathryn Swenson.

Mrs. Miller is the daughter of the B. Webbs. Webb will be in Houston to participate in a symposium concerning the exhibit to be held Monday at the Museum of Fine Arts in Houston.

Works shown are large outdoor contemporary sculpture, some as large as 30 feet in length and 20 feet in height. The site, Kirby and San Felipe Drive, is on a business thoroughfare so motorists and pedestrians can see the sculpture. Special illumination is installed for nighttime.

These art works by eleven nationally known artists will remain on site until Jan. 1. Artists include Antonakos, Bladen, Chamberlain, Henry Jimenez, Judd, Kipp, Meadmore, Murray, Surls and Woitena.

Participants in the symposium consist of artists, architects and museum directors. The exhibition is endorsed by Sen. John Tower, Mayor Fred Hofheinz, the Museum of Fine Arts and the Contemporary Arts Museum. Mrs. Miller is director of the Monumental Sculpture Appreciation Association, Inc.

Mimi Organizes Sculpture Exhibit. *Courtesy of the Wichita County Archives.*

Mimi was getting excited about organizing the installation. In 1975, she got permission from the River Oaks Bank to use a vacant area next to the bank for the exhibition: a two-acre lot at the corner of Kirby and San Felipe.

Knowing that, to be successful, her sculpture exhibition would have to showcase the known luminaries of the genre and that it would consume a lot of time, Mimi needed help. Browsing through her mental catalog of energy-driven, art-loving friends, she enticed well-known gallery owner Kathryn Swenson to join the project. Kathryn handled the money and helped her put things together. Mimi also remembered Eugene Binder, who was working in Dallas with Chapman Kelley, and hired him. Local artists also pitched in.

The bank's popularity already drew people to the area, which provided free advertising. Interested visitors could easily drive around the property and view the work. In addition, there would be a seminar at the Museum of Fine Arts, Houston where the artists would discuss their work with local patrons. And there would be a public discussion about the exhibit when everything was installed.

Mimi began the search for the best of the best, and twelve nationally recognized artists agreed to show their work in a three-month exhibition. The group included Stephen Antonakos, Ronald Bladen, Luis Jiménez, Donald Judd, Lyman Kipp, Clement Meadmore, James Surls, and John Chamberlain.

Mimi was anxious to meet all the people she'd studied in school at SMU. It was hard to believe they'd come down for her project, but they did!

John Chamberlain accepted the invitation, but his work failed to arrive. His friend and supporter, Stanley Marsh, who was asked to send the sculpture, instead sent two junk cars and a box of random parts, including a stuffed monkey's head, as a practical joke. The junk mimicked Chamberlain's style.

The man they hired to bring it back gave it to Dick Miller, who said it was a white '55 Chevy and some other stuff. It was not what Mimi told him the piece looked like. Workers had to take it off the field because it was not the right artwork. It wasn't even a work of art!

"It was all hilarious," Mimi told me, "except that we lost over $1,600 trying to get the Chamberlain sculpture to Houston." Mimi never received reimbursement from Stanley Marsh.

She was thrilled, however, as the other artists began to send their works.

Her father had agreed to come to Houston, providing a truck and a driver that brought James Surls's work. It was mostly made of wood, and it was big. Resembling a rounded log, it had spikes all over it. Mimi's dad said it reminded him of a Normandy minefield tank trap. She said she had no idea what that meant.

Mark di Suvero walks with a bad limp because he once fell down an elevator shaft. But he is one of the best artists in the country, according to Mimi. He did huge outdoor sculptures in New York City—one in each borough—when monumental art was just starting to become popular. Now, he came and helped the other artists, most of whom he knew, install their work.

Luis Jiménez showed up in an old pickup truck with a fiberglass sculpture of an Indian on a horse shooting a buffalo—and got stuck in the mud.

"It was a mess," Mimi said. "We were opening the next day. He had his wife with him. You could see their relationship wasn't great. It was my first time meeting him, and I liked his work."

Mimi told Luis that she had to defend him in Houston because when they unloaded his statue, Mrs. George Brown, a well-known philanthropist, created a row. According to Mimi she said, "You can see the Indian's testicles!" And indeed, you could. The Indian had a flap over his front and back that was flying high and exposing his privates.

Even though Mrs. Brown complained, Mimi was not rattled because Jiménez was an acclaimed sculptor with artwork at the Corcoran and the National Gallery of Art, among others.

There were other obstacles to overcome. It rained the day before the opening. As Mimi recalls, "I got Armco Steel to donate the hot-rolled steel for Donald Judd for four eight-foot-by-eight-foot boxes. He wanted a five-eighths-inch distance between each one. The rain had changed the ground. He showed up just as one of the boxes was dropped from where it was being installed by the forty-foot crane. I was just so horrified that he had to watch it. We had to wait to install the part later when it dried out because of the tiny space between the pieces."

After the crane operator dropped Judd's big box, Mimi sat on the street corner and cried. Don came over and said, "Do you want to smoke a joint?" Mimi responded, "'I guess so.' And he goes, 'It's ok, it's ok. It's going to be ok. It won't be any problem.'" She told me he made her feel wonderful.

The next morning it was still raining. And other disappointments rolled in. The Texas Southern marching band, "Ocean of Soul," was scheduled to perform but had to cancel due to the rain. Mimi's friend Eugene Binder bundled up and went home to Dallas because of prior work commitments. He missed the delayed official opening. Mimi had less help then and did not realize how tired she'd become.

The day that the exhibition was to open, it was still raining, and Dick went to clean up one of the exhibition sites and found it covered with fire ants. He got bitten, and his throat began to swell. Lyman Kipp from New York saw him stagger down the street and immediately called an ambulance.

Mimi described what followed. "My parents and sisters drove up at that moment, and my dad tore ass after them to Herman Hospital. Dick went into the ICU. My dad and I hadn't spoken in three years, but here he was, driving into Herman Hospital asking about his 'son.' And my dad said to me, 'Get in the car, Honey.' So here we are in Houston, which Daddy didn't know anything about, and how we got to the f******g hospital, I don't know, but we got there. The 'my son' comment blew me away."

Mimi saw her husband go into the ICU, and she saw him there with his blue jeans on. He had heard that fire ants attack your balls, so he was very concerned!

Unfortunately, Dick had to be in the hospital the next day, missing the symposium at the museum. Mimi could see him every three hours. She would head to the museum to be with the sculpture artists on the panel, ask a question, and then scurry back to the hospital.

The panel consisted of twelve artists plus major patrons, including Clement Meadmore, James Surls, John Henry, and Luis Jiménez.

Mimi looked out at the audience at the Museum of Fine Arts, Houston, and she observed all the people from Los Angeles and New York, as well as her dad. The celebrities included Peter Plagens—a big art critic. During the panel discussion, James Surls wore a huge button featuring Tom Hayden, a New Left political activist, horrifying her dad. But Bob Webb, the landscape architect, spoke Japanese and had previously worked with Japanese artist Isamu Noguchi. "So, Daddy understood the art world to some degree," Mimi told me.

Sometime after the symposium, the rain ceased, and the soil dried enough for the Judd boxes to be put into position, and the opening was scheduled for the next day.

Even though the exhibit opened later than anticipated, there was much fanfare, with Mayor Fred Hofheinz declaring it "Monumental Art

Day" in Houston. Mimi was very excited about the number of people attending. She told me that the event was even covered by the *Today Show.*

"It was a lot of work! The whole thing cost me over $260,000." Mimi told me that she paid for the artists to bring their work and for the cost of their trips to Houston.

All of this activity resulted in an invitation from pioneer public art champion Doris Freedman to come to New York City. "We had breakfast together," Mimi told me. "And I went to see every big-time art collector." They were curious about this new young person on the art scene that seemingly bloomed overnight. Mimi thought it overwhelming. "I went from one 5th Avenue apartment to another, meeting people. I think they were checking me out! I was new. People were thinking, 'What can we do with her?'"

In a contemporary interview with James Surls, he volunteered that Mimi had impressed the art world. She was viewed as an up-and-comer, smart and very capable.

Her reaction to the trip was fresh all these years later. "Oh my God—what a neat thing. I did not realize that it costs a lot of money, particularly to live there. I could tell she was a collector. And they had no idea I was as young as I was and that I didn't have all the money in the world." Clement Meadmore, who created the *Curl* sculpture on Columbia University's campus, once invited Mimi to teach his class there one evening. Afterward, he cooked dinner for his students.

On returning to Houston in mid-February, Mimi heard that Surls's thirty-foot wood sculpture had been vandalized. A businessman jogging in the predawn hours had noticed the fire. That terrified everybody. The artists panicked and began removing their work from the exhibition.

In a telephone interview in 2024, Surls told me that the act was clearly arson because gasoline had been poured down the middle of the work, titled *Point to Point*. He suspects that an uninvited artist was the culprit. The press called the event "a trash fire." Mimi believes some youths started the fire.

Mimi described it this way: "When the sculpture was vandalized, everyone wanted their sculpture, and we closed down. I had made one payment on insurance, which was expensive, but it covered everything. I think the show was up for six weeks instead of three months. During the shortened viewing time, no more harm was done."

Amid all the hoopla, Mimi's marriage to Dick wavered. For one thing, Mimi's husband did not get along with the artistic crowd. He could not follow the conversations and felt shunned. In addition, she'd married him when she was young. And Dick was an alcoholic. This made life together difficult. Soon, Dick and Mimi gave up living together.

Mimi moved into her office in Montrose right behind the River Oaks Bank building. She put her extensive collection of art and books into a storage garage about the time Houston became the victim of one of the worst floods in the city's history. The storage garage was inadequate to protect against the onslaught of wind and water. "I watched as the water of this monsoon covered the chairs and crept higher and higher," she told me. It was a steady scramble to protect her valuable art and records. "I cried because I knew I had to get it together and do something," she said.

And do something she did. After she divorced, she took the last part of the money she inherited from her grandfather to use for upcoming projects.

Next, Mimi approached Rice University again, this time looking to be an employee rather than a student. She was hired to work with the Rice University Art Gallery, whose collection included artists like Man Ray. It was a dream job for Mimi. The new head of the art department, Dominique de Menil, was running the museum, and Mimi loved Mrs. de Menil and what she was doing with the various artists.

Marian (Poo) Tower will be studying at the Sorbonne in Paris this spring semester, in SMU's foreign language program. She is the daughter of Lou Tower and Sen. John Tower, and granddaughter of Mr. and Mrs. Grover Bullington. . . Mimi Webb Miller of Houston, another granddaughter of the Bullingtqn's, is teaching modern art at Rice University. Also she and a friend have started a tour conducting agency in Houston, in which they give all day tours in the city. Mimi was here at Christmas to visit her grandparents, Mrs. Irene Webb and the Bullingtons, and her parents, Mr. and Mrs. Robert Webb.

* * *

Mimi Teaches Art at Rice University. *Courtesy of the Wichita County Archives.*

Mimi continued art consulting for big companies in downtown Houston, as she had before her exhibition. She drove a Mercedes at the time since Dick sold used cars. And she kept the Miller name. "It was such a hard thing to change," she told me.

She moved into a house on Albans Road behind Ouisie's Table in University Park with Sabra Smith, whom she had met at SMU. It was a beautiful place with many trees and a feeling of spaciousness. They lived together for several years.

Several years before, the de Menils had transferred their patronage from the University of St. Thomas to Rice, along with their art library and several staff members. Mimi had studied many of the artists that the de Menils brought to Houston and loved the chance to help Mrs. de Menil show off the collection. Mimi helped hang shows and give lessons to students. The job also had other advantages: she got to eat lunch with the teachers and visiting artists. Soon, she was organizing exhibitions for Houston galleries. Through her contacts at Rice, Mimi met many famous artists, including Andy Warhol. "Big people," she said. They impressed her because she had not seen art patrons connected with a university before.

She also started a company called Art Tours, taking people on tours of significant exhibitions. Later, Mimi expanded her offerings beyond

Page 10E Wichita Falls Times Wichita Falls, T

About people, places and things

By ANNIE LEE TERRY
Travel Editor

MUSEUM TOUR

The Wichita Falls Museum and Art Center is offering a tour to San Francisco in May, to see "The Splendors of Dresden." The exhibition, from Germany, covers five centuries of art collecting and contains more than 700 master works. Unlike most exhibitions, this is not a display of individual treasures, but instead it tells the story of the collecting of art as it developed in one dazzling baroque city, Dresden. Larry Francell, director of the Museum, said the tour will be May 11-15, and those who want to go should get in their reservations no later than April 10. The tour has been planned and will be directed by former Wichitan Mimi Webb Miller of Houston, daughter of the Bob Webbs.

Mimi Conducts Museum Tour. *Courtesy of the Wichita County Archives.*

Houston, including her hometown, Wichita Falls. Her company gave the tours in five languages. She also hosted a radio program.

Among Mimi's many friends, Bill Kugle, a lawyer from the East Texas town of Athens, was special. She began dating him when she was working at Rice.

Kugle was also a close friend of Ann Richards, a future Democratic governor of Texas. He took Mimi to a party in Temple in 1972 and introduced her to Ann. Mimi described the event to me.

"John Henry Faulk (the Texas Radio Star) was part of the group. I sat between him and Kugle, with Ann on the other side of Kugle. This is how Ann and I met. I heard her tell him, 'I cannot talk to your teeny bopper about her nail polish.'" Indignant, Mimi recalled this incident vividly. "I thought, God! I bite my nails. I never wear polish." Ann must have left about this time. Faulk leaned over to Mimi and said, "I know you are carrying 'an extra special cigarette.' Go outside where they are all smoking and talk with Ann."

Kugle asked her to step out on the porch and deliver some of those incentives (the marijuana joints) to move things along—the alcohol wasn't getting the job done! When she left the table, Kugle explained their relationship to Ann. Mimi elaborated, "I went out there, and everyone just grabbed for a joint. We all mellowed. By the time we came back in, everything was fine."

When Mimi returned, Ann Richards commented to Kugle, "I guess she will fit in." And she did, soon accompanying Ann to float through the lower canyons in the Big Bend of Texas. It was to be the start of a whole new adventure for Mimi.

CHAPTER 5

Big Bend Calling

Mimi had never traveled to Far West Texas, much less with many Democrats. However, when Bob Armstrong, the Texas land commissioner, put a list together with the help of Ann Richards, Mimi was invited along with Bill Kugle and many of the top Democratic leaders in the state. Bob touted the late-November event as a celebration of the inclusion of much of Big Bend National Park in the Interior Department's designation of the Rio Grande as a Wild and Scenic River. Mimi was delighted to be going along and was assigned to cook the turkey for the meal at the end of the trip.

It was all political. Ann had her eyes on running for governor, and all the big Democratic supporters were there.

The lower canyons of the Big Bend are truly beautiful, and the river, at lower levels, provided a stimulating ride for experienced rafters. Fortunately, Armstrong was such a person and made a hit with Mimi by extracting her several times from the uncaring rapids. Both Mimi and Kugle emerged from the experience thrilled beyond belief, and Mimi decided that this was to be the beginning of a love affair with the Big Bend.

At the end of the trip, with the turkey consumed, Ann, Bob Armstrong, and the other big-time Democrats went to a reelection fundraising party for Texas House Representative Buddy Temple in the Far West Texas towns of Study Butte and Marathon. Mimi was getting soaked with the Democratic political agenda, which interfaced nicely with the politics that she had been washed in during her stint in California.

On one of Mimi's rare returns to Wichita Falls in March following the opening of the Houston exhibition, she told her firmly Republican father that her political sympathies had changed. "I was so excited that Ann had organized that trip, so when I went home, I knew I couldn't be a Republican anymore. I really like the Democrats. They go to the river, get drunk, and tell wonderful stories. That was what kept me—that did it: their lifestyle, the way they lived life."

Mimi's trip to the Big Bend with Ann and the Dems was so much fun that she decided to give herself a Big Bend vacation. About six months after the trip with Ann, she went back to the Big Bend by herself. It was her first vacation trip alone since leaving Wichita Falls as a girl bound for college. To help her get ready, her dad gave her an axe, knife, heavy jacket, and cook stove.

"I'm an outdoor person. I fell in love with the country and came out for my first vacation as a single female alone—and then ended up coming out about once a month to break the routine of Houston."

Mimi told me that one of the first people she met in the Big Bend was Mike O'Connor. He had also taken a room at the hotel in Lajitas and dated an attorney in Alpine, Liz Rogers. The couple was well-known in the area. Mimi was eager to gain some social capital if she was to be spending time in the Big Bend.

"On my second trip west," Mimi recalled, "I went to Presidio, drove into the Presidio Grocery Store, and said I'm looking for Mike. I'd forgotten his last name. But I knew his business was liquid mix cattle feed. They told me where he was, so I started back toward Lajitas, got to a big field, and saw what looked like a gas container. I thought he said it was a round cylinder thing. He was feeding the cattle."

Mike told me, "I remember her crawling through the fence, which was astonishing as she was wearing a skirt."

When Mimi decided to develop friendships or anything else, she didn't dilly dally. Skirts and barbed wire never stopped her!

Back in Houston, Mimi was constantly working on one project or another. The monumental sculpture show had put her on the cultural map in the city despite the rain and fire accompanying the exhibition—even though the work was on display only for the better part of two months. People began to seek her advice on various projects, and she met many photographers, artists, sculptors, and arts writers.

In 1977, she was approached by an award-winning *Houston Chronicle* photographer, Blair Pittman, to assist in an arts project in Lajitas. A Houston developer, Walter Mischer, was looking to spread his investments beyond Houston and had conceptualized an adventure in the wilderness of the Big Bend, where he was constructing a romantic hotel and golf course to serve elite Texans eager to escape the banal pleasures of chain hotels.

For Mimi, this opportunity was a perfect fit. She envisioned exhibitions by nationally known artists, held in a location that combined the allure of Cancun or Cozumel with the mystery of abandoned mines, Indian trails, and the Rio Grande—welcoming visitors into Mexico.

Mimi thoroughly enjoyed selecting the artistic material for Pittman and set her sights on working directly for Mischer. The idea of an art gallery in the hotel was already taking shape in her mind.

On a trip to Lajitas, she entered the hotel restaurant for lunch and met the manager, Sheila, with whom she became friendly during her visits to the area. Sheila mentioned that Mr. Mischer was having drinks with friends at the bar, and Mimi walked over to his table, intending to introduce herself to him.

She approached the most distinguished looking of the men, believing he was Mischer. Instead, it was his son. After some confusion and laughter, she finally connected with Walter Mischer. They chatted, and Mischer suggested she give him a call when she got back to Houston.

So when she got home, Mimi wasted no time in contacting Mischer. It wasn't long before she was working directly for him at his new hotel, The Badlands, in Lajitas. After a couple of years, she got crosswise with coworkers and went to work as a cashier for Bill Ivey at his trading post in Terlingua. Ivey provided accommodations that she shared with another employee. Pittman writes that he first met Mimi while working as a photographer with the *Houston Chronicle.* He trusted her to lead him to important collectors. They worked well together.[1]

After trips to Lajitas and nearby Terlingua, Mimi had become consumed by the land. She reveled in the freedom she felt. No bustling traffic, no tall buildings disgorging thousands of people morning, noon, and night. She had a clear view to absorb the many mountain vistas around her. She decided this was where she wanted to live for a while.

Mimi had cashed out her remaining savings and inheritance, sold the Mercedes, and bought a red Checker cab that she could load full of gear. "I still have the Checker cab parked in front of my house in Ghost Town. It has become sort of a personal symbol," Mimi said.

Still, there were more things Mimi needed to learn as she undertook her Big Bend adventure. She described one lesson in particular, back in Houston. "I had a gun, but I couldn't get the safety off. I didn't understand it. So, I went by to see John Bintliff, a photographer I used to go out with, who was having a big party."

Bintliff showed her how it worked and then said, "That guy in the back room needs a ride to the Big Bend. I wonder if you can help him. He must rent a plane if you can't take him tonight." The man was Robert Chambers.

Mimi had begun to meet a variety of people like none she had encountered in the big cities. But she had yet to conquer the delusion of first appearances. After living with an organized, goal-driven man and then an alcoholic, she shifted to the attraction offered by handsome, forceful types.

Robert Chambers appeared to be such a man. Wearing a black leather trench coat and black workman's boots, Mimi thought he was the cutest thing in the world.

Even so, she was not thrilled at first about traveling a long distance with this unfamiliar man. "He doesn't even talk," she thought. Twelve hours in a car together is a long time, but he was attractive, so she agreed.

"We drove from Houston to the big hill at the Rio Grande River. It was dark when we got there, and I only saw the lower canyons. I didn't see all of it. We got out of the car, and he said, 'Follow me up this trail now.' I didn't know what we were up to. It was not connecting. Then he opened his briefcase and asked, 'Would you like to do a line?' I said, 'It's not really me.'"

Mimi realized, "He was not an artist. Robert was a cocaine dealer."

Somewhat later, he wanted to take her to Ojinaga, Mexico, just across the border from Lajitas. By this time, Mimi had relaxed somewhat in Robert's company. She had gotten to know him better, and he fascinated her with his stories.

One evening while Mimi and Robert were soaking up the late-evening sky near a lake, a man came up behind Robert. He leered at Mimi with teeth outlined in gold and asked in Spanish, "Is she your girlfriend?" Robert said, "No, I've just met her, and we're traveling around. That's her car." This was the first time Mimi Webb Miller conversed with Pablo Acosta Villarreal.

Terrence Poppa describes Pablo's appearance in his book *Drug Lord: A True Story*: "Pablo looked like he hadn't washed for two weeks. His skin was blotchy, his teeth misaligned, his nose was a real honker." Mimi, Poppa writes, thought he was ugly.[2]

Still, she was intrigued by him. "So, I knew Pablo for a long time," Mimi told me. "We were good friends. Our relationship deepened in the last year of his life, and we became very close. I liked him, and he liked me. We could talk for hours. He would talk about history and life in the Big Bend. I just ate it up. The last year of his life was real special."

While getting acquainted in Lajitas, Mimi continued to see Robert Chambers.

"He would stop by occasionally and visit," she told me. "One time, his motorcycle broke down, and he was afraid to get on it, thinking the Mexicans had fixed it so that he'd be embarrassed, and it would be broken. As you can imagine, he did a lot of business in Mexico."

But the more she got to know Robert, the less she liked him. She said he was abusive, and she was determined to get away from him.

"One day, he came to my apartment in Lajitas to take me to a Valentine's dinner the teachers at the school had thrown. It was outside near the school, and around eighty people were there. I made a cake and got a new shirt with hearts or something red on it. By the time we got as far as the airstrip at Lajitas, he already had the car door open and tried to push me out. I didn't want to go to the party anymore; I wanted Robert to disappear. I just wanted to go to my place. That didn't happen. We went to his place and drove past it. I didn't know where it was. He parked his Suburban, and it was dark. I didn't know what he was doing. He must have looked around to see if anyone could have seen us. Then he threw me into a ditch. He had hit me pretty hard, and I was bleeding. I went to talk to the law, but no one would help me.

"Another time, Robert broke my collarbone. I went to a doctor in Marfa, and he said, 'I know who did this to you, and he'll do it again.'"

Meanwhile, after spending time with the Mexican American artist Luis Jiménez, who had been part of her sculpture exhibition in Houston, Mimi began to immerse herself in the Mexican culture. She developed a love for crossing the Rio Grande year-round by boat or vehicle, depending on the depth of the water. She then drove the short distance to the village of San Carlos to enjoy all-night rancheros and watch cockfights. Her straw-blonde hair and light skin stood out from the black-haired crowd of Mexicans, who pestered her with offers of marriage and eternal love.

"Of course, I grew up with Mexican men," Mimi said. "My dad had seventy to eighty men who worked for him. I was not intimidated or uncomfortable around them."

At a cockfight one night in "no man's land" (a place in the middle of the river where there was no Mexican or American jurisdiction), a curly-haired Mexican caught her eye, and she accepted his offer to "show her around." They began to meet, and before long, Mimi's vaquero friend, Meño, became her common-law husband. He persuaded her to buy a ranch available a stone's throw across the border from Lajitas. Because Mexican law prohibited foreigners from owning land within fifty miles of the country's border, she put the property in the name of Meño's half-brother. The ranch was lovely! Eleven miles from Lajitas and 5,500 feet up a 6,000-foot mountain, it was 3,500 acres of land with a stream of spring water that poured from a forty-foot waterfall. It produced the best drinking water in Chihuahua. Mimi's new home sat near the waterfall.

In 1981, at age thirty-two, Mimi began living the Mexican life, naming her new acquisition the Miracle Ranch, or *Rancho El Milagro*. She quickly filled it with her collection of art.

Carlton Leatherwood describes the life Mimi enjoyed with Meño. He observed Mimi rolling flour tortillas in the kitchen of Rancho El Milagro. With no running water or electricity, life was simple.[3]

"The rocky road from the Rio Grande to Rancho El Milagro was passable year-round except when it rained, but it didn't rain very often," Mimi said.

The water of the Rio Grande spread like a moving sheet across an exposed slab of rock between Lajitas and the Mexican village of Paso Lajitas. It was one of several locations Native Americans used to move across the river for daily activities. The crossing also made for easy transport of stolen goods and booty from Mexico during the Indian wars with the Mexicans and the Comanche. It also served (and now serves) as a popular migrant crossing point.

"Soon after I moved to the ranch," Mimi told me, "I had a disaster. I was out milking goats and stepped on a four-inch nail. Of course, it hurt, but it was no big deal. I had over 200 goats that I had been milking, so I didn't go to a doctor immediately."

It turned out to be a really big deal. Mimi finally went to El Paso, where she consulted doctors, including Dr. Lee with whom she was familiar. But no one could figure out the problem, and Mimi spent three and a half months in the hospital's terminal ward. Dr. Lee would bring her art that she would tape to the wall and the ceiling. Mimi would take the empty injection syringes, wash them out, fill them with glitter or sequins, and send them to friends. She didn't have much else to do. Often, her temperature would spike, and there would be a frantic rush to control it. Once it hit 104 degrees. She said later that she was near death.

Mimi had about ten operations on her leg. "It's real from here to there," she indicated, showing me. "To here and underneath." The doctors would slice it open and remove tissue each time. Finally, she received a diagnosis. It was a bacterial infection: Mycobacterium tuberculosis. Hers was the only case in the United States.

"When they came to talk to me about it, I said, 'Why are you asking me all these questions? It's not in my chest; it's in my foot!' I couldn't figure out what they were trying to get to. John Tower found some experts, so I went to Dallas for the last operation. My aunt came and picked me up."

Mimi continued: "This infectious-disease guy came in and said, 'We are going to cut you open, and we're gonna cut out that area because there is no one else in the United States that has that disease. There are three Haitians with Mycobacterium tuberculosis. We don't want it to spread here.'"

Mimi took some heavy-duty pills and then headed home. "I had taken the bus to get to Alpine," she recalled, "and I thought Meño was going to be picking me up there, but he didn't, and I was pissed off and walked to the outskirts of Alpine with my crutches on and a big cast. I knew nearly everybody who passed by, but no one would stop. Finally, some guys stopped and said, 'Oh, we'll take you.'"

Well, they were a couple that drank, and when they opened their ice box, there was ice, bourbon, and all sorts of stuff. Mimi was grateful for a share of their beverages and explained that Meño was supposed to meet her and didn't. They knew what was happening. Meño's behavior was common knowledge. The men just got drunker and drunker, waiting to see how things would play out. As it turned out, Meño was at another woman's apartment. Mimi figured out where it was and banged on the door. After that, she ended up living at the ranch alone.

Eventually, Pablo Acosta became a frequent visitor to Mimi's ranch, even before he took over the Ojinaga plaza and became the underworld power in the area. The first time he visited, he arrived with the usual display of weapons and the typical entourage of *pistoleros*. He and his men lounged around in the shade of the patio. Meño had dealings with Pablo and, during those dealings, had begun to shoot up heroin.

In Jefferson Morgenthaler's *The River Has Never Divided Us*, we get a clear picture of Pablo's weaknesses. Naturally, drugs. Specifically, crack cocaine. Alcohol and some pot, too, but "Mood swings, feelings of invincibility, loss of perspective, fear of conspiracies" made the cocaine addiction deadly. "His second deadly attraction was to Mimi Webb Miller." More on that a bit later.[4]

Around this time, Mimi was also getting better acquainted with the artist Luis Jiménez. She was impressed not only with his work but also with his personality. In addition, they shared a mutual respect for common, hard-working people. Jiménez had grown up working in his father's sign manufacturing business, making neon tubing in multiple colors, and started his career teaching art in public schools.

When Mimi bought the ranch in Mexico, Jiménez sent her a painting that she framed and hung in her new house. "I have a whole series of his work," she told me. On the framed work that he made while she was living in Mexico, she took a magic marker and colored on the glass. "I made the man in the painting look like a Mexican because everyone was coming and asking, 'Is that Robert?'"

Luis had come with two helpers to move Mimi out of Bill Ivey's trading post, and by that time, she had fallen in love with Meño and was moving to Mexico. But "Luis would come by every once in a while and stay with me. He finally broke up with his wife. I could tell they weren't happy together."

Soon, the acquaintance became more serious. "Over the years, we had this ongoing affair," Mimi told me. She said they dated until he died in 2006. "He and I had been talking quite a bit before he died. A thirty-two-foot-tall piece, *Blue Mustang*, fell from a hoist in his Hondo, New Mexico, studio, severing an artery in his leg. His children were in the room. Horrifying."

The completed work now stands near the Denver International Airport.

Still traveling to Houston on occasion for work, Mimi one time brought a goat to Houston from the ranch so Meño could do a goat roast. "We set up in the backyard, and Meño began to sever the goat's head from its body," Mimi recalled. There was much commotion as the kicking goat protested his sacrifice. It also slung a red cloud over the backyard. Once the neighbors understood what was happening, they became unglued. "Two priests came and talked with me," Mimi recalled.

CHAPTER 6

Pablo

Pablo Acosta and his organization, meanwhile, were growing more powerful. So in 1983, the U.S. Customs Narcotics Service sent federal agent David Regela to break up the cartel. Acosta had been "well documented as an extremely dangerous and ruthless fugitive, who has been responsible, either directly or indirectly, for in excess of twenty murders." Regela met Mimi when he arrived on the border (to focus on Pablo Acosta) and was immediately taken by her knowledge of the area and her good looks. It wasn't long before they were dating.[1]

Regela admits his intimate connection with the woman he called "the queen of the borderlands" in his book, *Against the Wind*.[2]

In December of 1976, David Regela earned a reputation for being a forceful agent. One night during a highly dangerous gunfight against three-dozen men carrying Winchesters and revolvers, Regela and other agents used the element of surprise as they leapt from their camper and attempted to capture the entire group.[3]

Meanwhile, Meño had been doing business with Pablo, and Pablo would occasionally stop by Mimi's ranch for short visits. One day, when she was alone at home, he grilled her about her association with Regela. Mimi calmed him down, responding, "You don't have anything to worry about. All he wants is to get into my pants."

Things were deteriorating between Mimi and Meño. Meño had been using drugs for a long time, even before he hooked up with Mimi. He always had an excuse for his behavior while under the influence. Mimi was getting tired of them. He claimed to have gotten hooked on heroin while packing the drug for shipment, saying it got under his fingernails and he had absorbed it through his skin. He had slowed down his usage when he first met Mimi, but the attraction of the drug was too strong, and he had begun abusing it again. Finally, Mimi told him to leave. It was over.

Mimi turned her concern to Pablo's exposure. She was pretty sure that he was trafficking drugs with others along the border.

As Poppa observed in his book, "The Pablo she knew didn't square with the DEA's characterization as a 'vicious, extremely dangerous person with very little regard for human life.'" The only side of himself that Pablo wanted her to see was "that of a champion of the poor, a man of honor who filled in for a rapacious government that was only interested in perpetuating itself at the expense of the people."[4]

Pablo admitted to doing some bad things but usually it was to help poor people. "People think I am a rich man," Pablo maintained, "that I make my money lying down. They are mistaken. . . . I don't even have a carport," he told one of his interviewers.[5]

Despite his own debilitating drug addiction, Pablo was so confident of his hold on the drug business that he was not afraid of the authorities. But many of his associates were losing faith in his leadership. Mimi was concerned that rival dealers, Mexican police, or American federal authorities would catch him open to the world. So, she arranged to have Pablo and Regela meet in Mexico, saying, "I want to get you two together." The head of the radio station in Ojinaga quickly gave up his office to Pablo and Regela. The three of them, Pablo, David, and Mimi, sat down and began to get acquainted. Mimi was with them for the thirteen-hour discussion.

Mimi thought that Pablo should give himself up to the Americans because they would put him away for a short time. A Colombian cartel was making attempts to move into his territory. Mexican police were after him. Either the rival cartel bosses or the Mexican government would kill him. But Pablo would not bring himself to submit to the authorities, even to save his life.

In 1985, *Washington Post* writer Walt Harrigan visited the Big Bend in an effort to learn more about the lawless West. He found that violence is normal along the border between the US and Mexico. When a man named Refugio Gardea Gonzalez "was busted out of . . . jail in his underwear" and "came to be hogtied and left [naked] at a roadside park," they were not overly concerned. When Sheriff Jones found him, Gonzalez was shouting, "Mafiosa, Mafiosa!"

Harrigan expands on his observations of colorful people on the border and gets around to meeting Mimi, of course. He learned that "the Mexicans call the beautiful women who lives alone in the Chihuahuan Desert 'La Gringa Guera'—the blond American."[6]

Harrigan concluded his report from the lawless West with great humor and a wink. On his way out of town, he took another swing past Acosta's house. Not at home. But a little way down the road he found Bob Dillard, the editor of *The Alpine Avalanche*. He asked, "You know who did it, don't you?" He nodded and smiled but concluded that no one will ever know for sure—unless he asks Acosta right out. When he does, he will "know by the smile on his face."[7]

As Mimi's relationship with David Regela faded into a friendship, Pablo and Mimi's relationship intensified. He moved Mimi into an Ojinaga apartment she paid for. She began spending a lot of time with him, using her place as essentially a safe house.[8] Pablo came only once to the apartment. "He was pretty opinionated, and we had wonderful talks," Mimi told me.

"As a result, David Regela became preoccupied with Mimi's safety. Amid scheming and intrigue, plots and counterplots, murders and attempted murders, she was naive and trusting. Regela could see that the blonde, Texas senator's niece had become enamored with the border drug baron."[9]

Regela continued to explain to her that an ambush attempt against Pablo would get her blown away as well if she were with him. He advised her that Pablo would not last the year against the Colombian cartel and other enemies he had developed. He wanted her to return to Wichita Falls until things settled down. And she did as he wished. For a while.

Mimi tipped off a couple of FBI agents from Miami to check out rumors of Libyan terrorists sneaking into the United States through the Big Bend and of terrorist training camps in northern Chihuahua. Pablo told the agents he had not heard about such camps—his people would have informed him of them. "To the astonishment of the FBI agents, Pablo volunteered to fight the terrorists if indeed there were any preparing to attack America. He didn't want anything to happen to the United States. He owed everything he had to the United States. . . . The FBI agents later

"Mexico is a one-party dictatorship," Poppa said. "It's been that way for six decades. And in the course of this six decades, not only has it become corrupt, it has become absolutely corrupt, and every kind of racketeering imaginable is practiced by the government of Mexico.

Poppa said his meeting with Acosta was arranged with the help of Acosta's neighbor, Mimi Webb-Miller, the niece of former U.S. Sen. John Tower of Dallas.

"I was pretty scared," Poppa recalled. "He had a reputation for being a vicious killer. In fact, one of the stories told about him was that he would cut (his victims) open after he'd kill them, put rocks in their body and then drag the body behind his (truck) through the desert until there wasn't much left of the body."

Acosta Meeting Arranged with Help of Mimi Webb Miller. *Courtesy of the Wichita County Archives.*

Pablo Acosta Portrait on Cover of Book by Terrence E. Poppa. *Photograph by Bill Wright.*

wrote back to Mimi that meeting Pablo had been one of the 'high points' of their long careers."[10]

Meanwhile, Pablo solicited Regela for the murder of Lupe Arevalo, assuring him that he would have plenty of money for life. Regela replied, "Pablo, I'm not an assassin."[11]

In 2005, I interviewed Robert Chambers's dad, Boyd, for my book

The Texas Outback: Ranching on the Last Frontier. My friend David Haines and I drove to the Chambers ranch headquarters, far up the Rio Grande River Road from the village of Candelaria, and asked Chambers to tell us about ranching in the far reaches of the Big Bend.[12]

I saw the new airstrip on the ranch as we drove in. The family was still concerned with the Border Patrol. At the time, I wondered if the airstrip was just for family, visitors, and businesspeople.

Boyd told me about the Customs problems at the time. "I've had migrants in the house; I haven't ever caught one uninvited. No confrontation with them. The worst thing I ever had was not the wetbacks but the Border Patrol. They thought they could do anything they wanted to do."

The day dragged to a close as Haines and I headed back to the river road, Candelaria, Presidio, and pavement to Marfa. As we passed the new landing strip, almost hidden in the mesquite and brush, we wondered if our new friend Boyd had a reason to be worried about the airplanes that seemed to create a vigil around his ranch. Our musing on the subject was brief, however, as we both became absorbed with the brilliance of the western sky in our rearview mirrors. It would break anyone's chain of thought.

However, I was unaware of Boyd's son's relationship with Mimi. I learned later that her intuitions about Robert had some merit. On December 3, 1991, federal agents were tipped off about a pickup truck containing drugs crossing the river near Presidio before daylight, and the next day, a horse trailer was found parked at the County Fairgrounds in Marfa that contained 2,400 pounds of pure cocaine. It turned out that the trailer was owned by the sheriff of Presidio County, Rick Thompson, and his partner in the affair was none other than the son of my new friend, the rancher I had interviewed, Boyd Chambers.

"In 1985, the El Paso Intelligence Center compiled a 223-page report of information on the Pablo Acosta organization. In that lengthy document, Pablo was described as vicious, ruthless, and extremely dangerous. His Mexican mafia was said to be five hundred strong."[13]

Terrence Poppa wrote the story of Pablo's exploits for the *El Paso Herald-Post* in the late 1980s.

"Now, Acosta is too dangerous for the Mexican authorities in Juárez to allow him to live. Acosta has smuggled over sixty tons of cocaine,

Mimi on Horseback. *(unknown photographer)*

Mimi with Two Men. *(unknown photographer)*

along with many tons of marijuana, into the U.S. every year. Sheriff Thompson and Robert Chambers, a cowboy and border ruffian from Alpine, Texas, are his secret minions, both playing vital roles in Acosta's border drug-smuggling empire and river-smuggling operations in the seven counties of Far West Texas."[14]

Mimi went to town to get help but discovered that Pablo had made a fast trip to Santa Elena, a village of three hundred people on the Rio Grande across from Big Bend National Park, to hide out. She immediately got in the Checker cab to head there. Before she crossed the river, she got stopped by the cops and assumed it was Customs. Fortunately, because she was in the Checker, they knew exactly who she was. Mimi left the Checker and took the boat across the river. One of Pablo's main guys, a good man with a good heart, met her. He said they were low on supplies and had twenty-two men guarding Pablo who needed food. She felt it was getting close to a shootout, but Pablo wanted to see her. She went to the adobe house in the center of the village where he was holed up with two bodyguards and found out it was the Mexican police who were coming for him. Pablo made it clear that he would not surrender. He knew the end was near.

Pablo's feet were severely swollen, and Mimi asked his men to get some cottonwood tree leaves to soak his feet with. She told them it would help reduce the swelling. They thought she was brilliant. They returned with baskets of leaves but not a single cottonwood leaf. Mimi decided to use anything they brought.

In his book *Drug Lord*, Terrence Poppa described the final day of Pablo's life with Mimi:

> Mimi spent all of Thursday morning with Pablo, and a part of the early afternoon, talking in the modest dining room-living room in the front of the mud brick house. Two of Pablo's nephews, . . .

from Odessa, Texas, hung around the kitchen as Pablo's personal bodyguards.

They talked about the strange things that had been happening at Mimi's ranch. Someone had driven by recently and machine-gunned the ranch house while no one was there. Then it was rumored that a criminal complaint had been filed in Chihuahua City accusing Pablo of the shooting. The complaint allegedly contained Mimi's signature. If it were true that such a document existed, it was absurd. Pablo theorized that someone wanted to kill Mimi and blame it on him. The fabricated complaint would serve as a pretext for accusing him. Pablo pleaded with Mimi to leave the borderlands entirely, to return to Wichita Falls and stay with her family.

"If you stay around here, they'll kill you and they'll kill you bad."

"What do you mean by 'kill bad,'" Mimi asked.

He shrugged his shoulders. "They'll make you hurt before they kill you." . . .

"You don't have to say any more," Mimi said, turning pale.

About two in the afternoon, Pablo told Mimi she had to leave.

They bade one another a tearful goodbye. One of the gunmen escorted her down to the river and stood on the riverbank as the boatman rowed her back across the Rio Grande.

Mimi had to walk up the dirt road to get to her car. She turned around before entering the thicket of mesquite trees and looked back at the river and at the high bluff on the other side that hid the village from view. She had a feeling that she was never going to see him again.[15]

Acosta was killed on April 24, 1987, by Mexican federal police, led by Comandante Calderoni. It was a fight to the death.[16]

After Pablo's death was confirmed, Sheriff Rick Thompson warned Mimi that there would be a price on her head because she knew so much about the cartel. David Regela suggested to her that it might be wise to move temporarily back to Texas from her ranch house as tensions were running high. He brought two armed Customs officers with him, and they moved all her furniture and art. Everything.

Mimi told me that she had a beautiful Frank Tolbert painting that got dipped in the river, but they got everything back across. Mimi didn't have a house in Terlingua at that time, so she loaded it all in a trailer. Of course, the Drug Enforcement Administration immediately and thoroughly searched through everything as soon as they were involved.

"When I came back over the river it was like I didn't know what was happening," Mimi said. "I just knew I needed to get out of that area. Pablo had been killed, and things were still trying to straighten themselves out."

Mimi gave me a full description of that day. Pablo's niece, Annette, who lived in Odessa, was sent by Pablo's mother to Mimi at the Lajitas Trading Post, saying they needed to go and pick up the body. Mimi got her car, and they drove into Big Bend National Park from Study Butte.

When they got into the park, Mimi could see Pablo's body bag because they were transferring it to Mexico. They had to stop in the US to refuel the helicopters used for transport. This was rough for her. There were two or three helicopters, and the place was packed with cops and military.

"There must have been fifty or so US people, and they all looked at me and the Checker cab. I mean all conversations stopped as I drove toward the helicopters and the body bag," Mimi said.

She could read their lips. "They said in unison, 'What the f*** is she doing here?'"

A man in an FBI jacket came over and quietly explained what was going on. They couldn't give up custody of Pablo's body because at this point it belonged to the Mexican military. Because they were on the American side, they were heading to El Paso with the body. Another FBI agent, Tom Farris, explained that the body would then be taken to Juárez and that they would have to go there to negotiate that issue. Mimi complained that Pablo was a naturalized American citizen, but it was to no avail.

There was nothing more she could do.

So, she started toward Wichita Falls with Tom Farris escorting her in his vehicle. Mimi told me they stopped at the Study Butte store, which was full of everybody talking about what was going on, so she went back and sat in the car because she couldn't take it. Tom said that she needed to get out of there and that he would call her family and say she was coming. She was driving so fast and crying so hard that at one point Tom pulled up next to her and said, "Let's get a beer." He got her as far as Odessa. Mimi said he was one of the kindest men she had ever met. She continued on toward Wichita Falls for about thirteen hours but got lost. It was after midnight when she got to her hometown.

Mimi gave me the following almost verbatim:

> Now, at home, I remember going into the kitchen and finding my dad eating. I have to tell you the one thing I remember. My dad always looked at me as fearless. I was the oldest, but I was also the more adventuresome. He even came down twice to Terlingua when I wasn't there to go to a wedding and hopefully meet Pablo. At another get-together, he didn't see Pablo but met Pablo's men.
>
> Then they put me to sleep in one of the bedrooms—I mean, you know, we were kids growing up there—so the house was big

and pretty empty then. And during the night, I heard something at the window. I got a gun. I am a good shot, and I immediately assumed somebody was trying to get in on the side of the house. My bedroom had always been at the front of the house, separate from everybody else, and then I was sleeping in the room my dad slept in, which was right next to mine. And he had gone back with my mom in the bedroom towards the back of the house, and so I got this gun, and I guess it was about a twenty-minute situation where I could hear things out the window, but I couldn't tell that there was anybody there. Finally, I opened it with the gun, ready to shoot right through it.

It was a moth.

Sandwiched between the window and the screen, the moth was wildly attempting to escape. I knew how the moth felt. The experience with the moth made me realize that I was in bad shape

Mimi's Red Checker Cab. *Photograph by Bill Wright.*

and needed some help. I had to take responsibility for protecting myself.

The next day, Mimi started looking for information about the Texas Health and Science Research Center in Dallas. They could offer her help for depression and trauma. She told her dad her plans, and he agreed that she was properly diagnosing herself. Mimi said, "In his heart, he felt I would be safer wherever the FBI told me to go." So, she got all dressed up, took some joints of marijuana with her, and headed off in the Checker cab to Dallas.

All she could think about was that she had no idea what was in front of her. She assumed that the center's staff would sit her down and talk. A counselor named John Rich called her.

"I know exactly who you are," Mimi said, and began describing her concerns.

John replied, "Mimi, our facility is not secure enough for you."

Instantly, all the fear came back to her. "I knew that would happen," she told me. "You could tell John was prepared for that."

She was on the verge of crying because she was so frightened, but John reassured her, saying, "I'm going to send you to a place in Fort Worth where you'll be safe."

"I think he said he was calling Customs," Mimi told me. "I gave him the copy of a letter I sent to Customs in case he needed to verify I wasn't crazy. I told him about the bad guys across the border and how I barely made it home, and now I don't feel safe again." Mimi confirmed that US Customs helped her get into the hospital.

John gave Mimi directions to the Fort Worth psychiatric hospital that was more secure. When she got close, she saw Mrs. Baird's Bakery and thought, "Oh my God, that must be where he wanted me to go, but no, it wasn't." Her mind was in a swirl. She kept driving until she saw the facility: a low-slung, contemporary building. She went to the back door, where staffers let her in and began talking to her. They were very concerned about the red cab in the parking lot so someone with Customs moved it. And they were concerned for her, understanding that she was just hanging on.

The hospital's counselor, Terry Anderson, asked Mimi, "Do you have a gun?"

"Yes."

"Where is it? Just tell us where it is, and we'll get it." Staff members were going through her bags. They got to the bottom of her suitcase and saw multiple boxes of hollow-point bullets. Every Border Patrolman had given her a box. Whenever she had a flat tire on the road to Ojinaga, Border Patrol would show up. Mimi stood out.

The hospital gave Mimi some sleeping medication and put her in a private room. The next day, she heard the door open quietly, and she sat straight up in bed, asking what the matter was. A staff member just wanted to tell her about the doctor. "What happened to the doctor?" she asked. Her mind raced through thousands of scenarios, including that maybe he was killed. The staffer told her he had to pay a traffic ticket. When she apologized for her reaction, they reassured her, telling her that it gave them helpful information about her. They talked to Customs and the FBI periodically. Mimi remembers that "they had a military guy who was a therapist, and he met me in a little room where I was staying. It had a Parsons table in it and two chairs."

"The military doctor started talking, saying, 'Well, just tell me what you think if you were trapped in a place underneath that Parsons table.' I thought, what a stupid f****** thing to say. I don't think I was really impressed with the program."

So, after five weeks, Mimi decided to go home. She couldn't afford to stay at the hospital anymore. They returned her small .380 gun and all her belongings when she checked out. Mimi was there between five and six weeks, "and when I got the first bill, it was $33,000, and I nearly had a heart attack," she said.

While home in Wichita Falls, Mimi helped plan her high school reunion. She also had a couple of really good friends there, and she was able to tell them a little about what had happened and why it was a bit of a mess.

Her friend, David Regela, summarized the cause of her new status due to her "proximity" to the now dead mafioso. "Mimi's only sin was an honest effort to humanize a man much of the world took great delight in demonizing and vilifying. Pablo's passing would, in fact, propel Mimi on her own dark journey of the soul."[17]

In an interview with *Oprah Daily's* Elena Nicolaou, we learn more about this season of Mimi's life even though her portrayal in Netflix's *Narcos: Mexico* is not completely accurate. "Played by Sosie Bacon, the 27-year-old daughter of acting legends Kevin Bacon and Kyra Sedgwick, Mimi Webb Miller is one of the newest—and most welcome—additions to the *Narcos* universe."[18]

Mimi knew she needed to get to a safer place. So, she decided to seek shelter among friends in El Paso.

CHAPTER 7

El Paso

In the late 1970s, my dad and I expanded Western Marketing, our petroleum products company, to El Paso. I regularly traveled from Abilene to monitor operations. I would fly there in my Cessna, spending a couple of days looking for new locations for service stations and a truck stop. Usually, I would swing by on the way and visit friends in the Big Bend area, and I was aware of the troubles Mimi had inherited. Visiting friends in Terlingua, I discovered that Mimi was living in El Paso. I decided to see if I could find her. I did, and to her surprise, I called and invited her to dinner one night while I was in town.

I met Mimi at a restaurant that she recommended, and we started talking. She revealed the circumstances that made moving necessary. Of course, I promised silence. I didn't want to see my friend become a victim of some retaliatory strike by the drug king's organization. We talked well into the night about the events of the past few years—the gun battle, Pablo's death, and what happened when she got the news.

Our conversation ended as I walked her to her Checker cab. Soon afterward, I heard that she had moved to California, and I lost contact with her except for a few letters.

Mimi had chosen to go to El Paso because Customs agent David Regela, whom she had dated back in the Big Bend, was living there with his wife. She certainly didn't want to stay in Wichita Falls. The moth incident in the window was enough. She didn't know who was looking for her. As far as the FBI was concerned, that was fine.

Regela was surprised to see Mimi walk into his office one day. "She looked worn, stressed, and considering the dire events of the last couple of months, that was to be expected. While Pablo Acosta had lost his life, Mimi had lost her lifestyle."[1]

While Mimi was in El Paso, Regela and another Customs officer took her to visit Guillermo González Calderoni, head of the Mexican federal police. His office was on the sixth floor of a tall building in Juárez, Mexico. Two officers in uniform and carrying guns accompanied the Americans.

Calderoni was a strange man with eyes that pointed in two different directions. He was ready for them with many questions.

"Come on in and tell me what you know, and you can go home," he said.

"Well, I wouldn't live very long if I did that!" Mimi responded. "I really don't know a bunch of stuff. It was a personal relationship, and I wasn't involved in any trafficking."

Calderoni said, "I wouldn't go back right now [to Lajitas]; it's too dangerous." He showed Mimi a picture of Pablo sitting in a bar with his arm around a woman. She thought he must have believed she would be jealous. Calderoni asked if she thought he was trying to get information on the gang that was taking Pablo's place, and Mimi replied, "I assume so."

The tension in the meeting could be cut with a knife. As the conversation continued, it became evident to Mimi that even El Paso was not a safe place for her, with a price on her head by Pablo's family, who initially thought she was responsible for his death. So, she decided to find a safer place to live until things cooled down.

Mimi and Regela left the office and headed for his vehicle, but Mimi was shaken by the visit with Calderoni and thought, "We had six people waiting for us in the parking lot, but what the f*** could they have done?"

As they pulled away, Mimi told David Regela, "I was pregnant, and

I lost the child." David asked if she was inferring that he was the father. She said, "Oh, no, no. It was Pablo's baby. I was at the ranch and lost the baby when the horse threw me." Pepe, the young brother on the adjacent ranch, was shooting at Mimi's dogs. "I landed hard. The horse was freaked out by the shot that came between me and his mare."

"That night, I lost the baby. I was about four and a half months pregnant. I didn't think I could get pregnant. I was thirty-seven and had endometriosis. I never worried about getting pregnant," she explained.

In a contemporary interview, Mimi and I revisited our conversation that evening in El Paso. She told me she did not have any other idea where to go. "At first I must have had money and stayed at a hotel—or with the Regelas; I don't remember. They had a condo on the west side of El Paso, which is nice. They both had good jobs."

Mimi had been in El Paso for a year, working as a waitress at Bennigan's. After our visit, her housing situation changed. The people moved out of the house she was living in, leaving her with their dog and a bunch of furniture, which she burned to stay warm. She didn't object to the dog because it provided some protection from the drug dealers who had been living in the house before her.

At this point Mimi just wanted out of El Paso and Texas. She had been recognized in the restaurant by some people from San Carlos. I asked her if the FBI chose where she would live. "No," she said. "But that's a good question. I had to ask them for some money. I think I asked the FBI when I went to California. But I had a college roommate in Venice, and I could go there and stay at her place. She would be gone for three months."

She still wasn't sure where she would feel safe, but she drove to California and parked the Checker in her friend's garage and began the next chapter of her life.

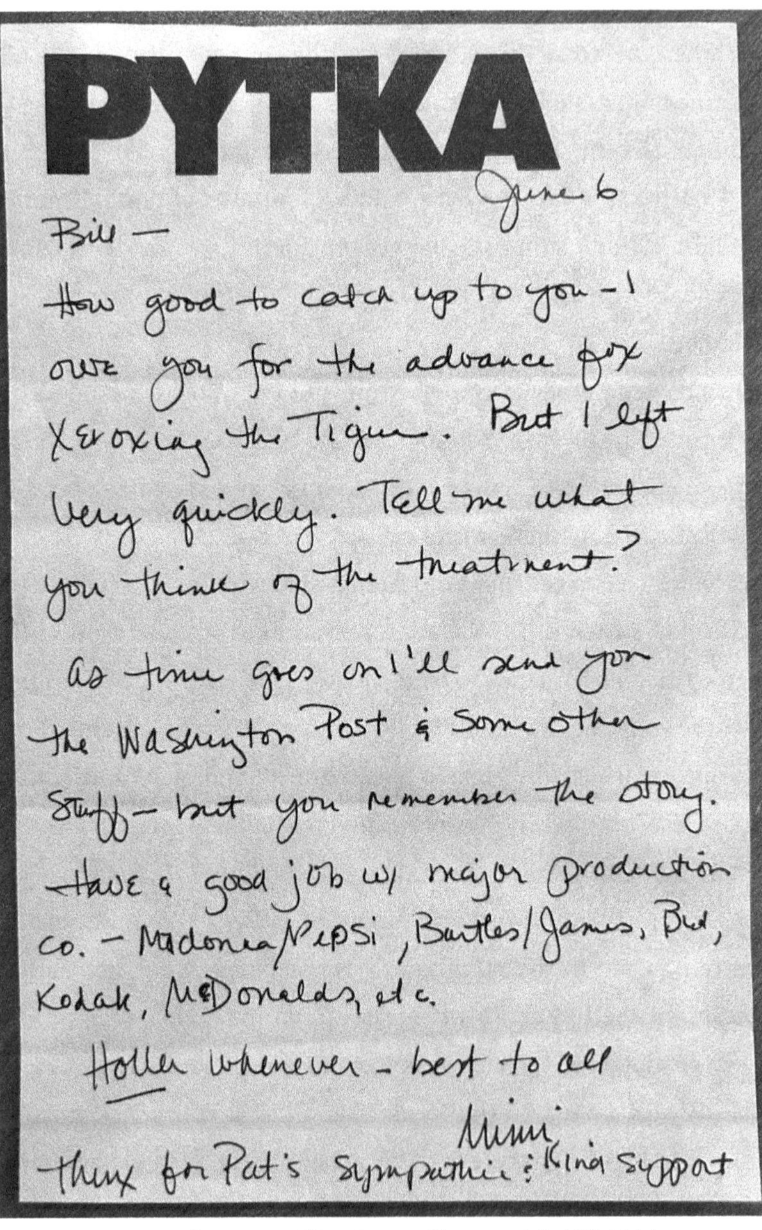

PYTKA

June 6

Bill —

How good to catch up to you – I owe you for the advance for Xeroxing the Tiger. But I left very quickly. Tell me what you think of the treatment?

As time goes on I'll send you the Washington Post & some other stuff – but you remember the story.

Have a good job w/ major production co. – Madonna/Pepsi, Bartles/James, Bud, Kodak, McDonalds, etc.

Holler whenever – best to all

Mimi

Thanx for Pat's sympathetic & kind support

PYTKA June 6 / Mimi's Note to Bill on June 6. *Photograph by Bill Wright.*

PYTKA

8-23

Bill —

Thanks <u>so</u> much for calling. I feel a lot less alone when I connect w/ my friends – I do miss the Southwest. LaLa land is a bit surreal – Venice is I guess a great place if one has to be here. I have a tiny place (which of course looks just like my ranch house inside) – but it has a neat back yard and I'm a blk off the beach.

Here is some of the "story" — But I feel a definitive version of <u>my</u> story will be out Oct in NY

PYTKA August 23 / Mimi's Note to Bill on 8/23. *Photograph by Bill Wright.*

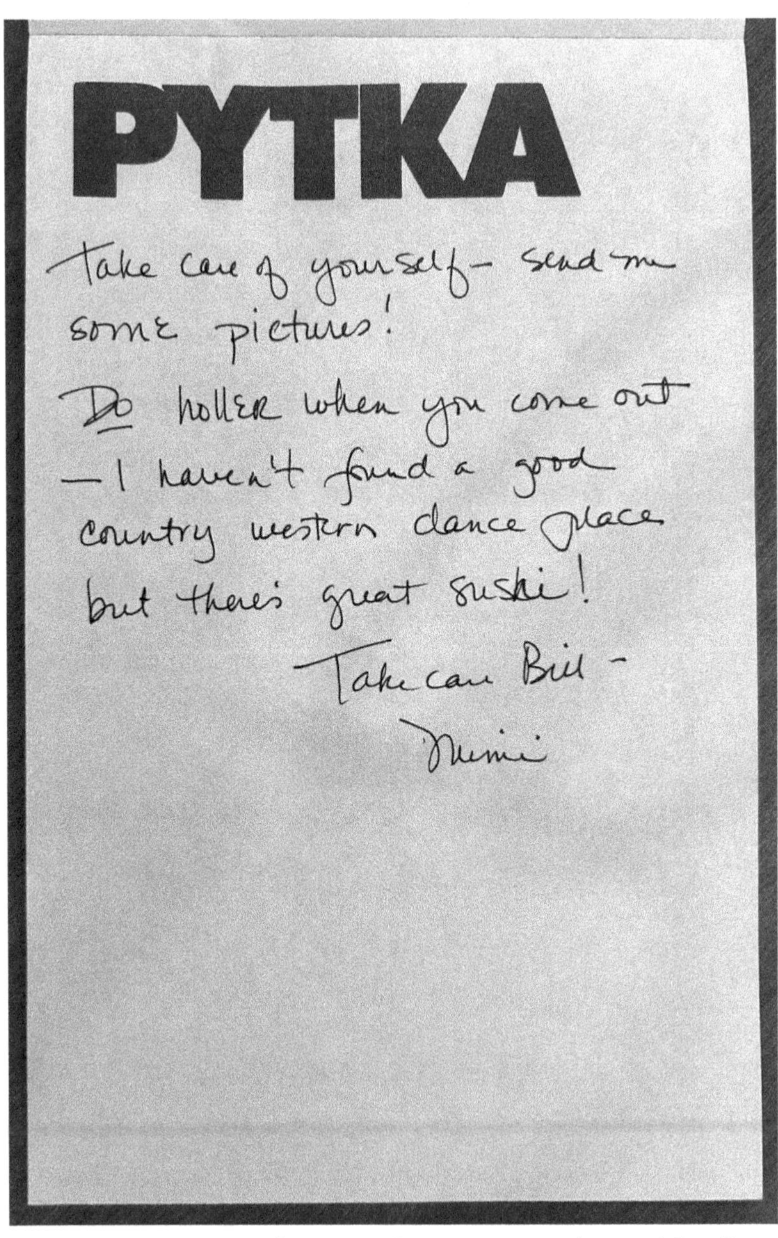

PYTKA

Take care of yourself– send me
some pictures!
Do holler when you come out
—I haven't found a good
country western dance place
but there's great sushi!
Take care Bill–
Mimi

PYTKA Take Care Bill / Mimi's Note to Bill on 8/23, page 2. *Photograph by Bill Wright.*

CHAPTER 8

California

Mimi was back in California, and the excitement she felt during her college years felt fresh again. For work, she got settled helping her lawyer friend, Valerie, whom she knew from Mills, who introduced her to people in LA who needed help with legal work. One task was vetting college applicants' credentials, like awards they received and clubs they belonged to. She would go through peoples' backgrounds so that they could be rated. Valerie paid her ten bucks an hour, "which was great," Mimi told me.

Finally, because her old college roommate was due back, Mimi found a new place to live across Pacific Avenue in Venice, which runs along the ocean: a little apartment at the back of a house that cost $400 a month to rent.

Mimi lived there over thirty-six years. "The whole backyard—you know my dad was a landscape architect—the backyard is f****** beautiful," she said. "There were five other apartments, all from around 1936—old places, but I felt pretty safe there."

Mimi heard from a friend, Cathi Carlton, whom she had met down in Big Bend, and who had gone to work in Venice for a guy named Joe Pytka. Pytka was a well-known director of commercials, music videos, and films. She found out that his office was three blocks away.

So, Mimi went and knocked on the door. She described that day.

> Now, mind you, I had a skirt on that had a huge hole I was hoping nobody would see. I mean, I had not spent much money on

> anything. A woman answered the door, and I said, "Is there a girl named Cathi Carlton here?" And she's looking at me, and it's just so weird: I'm standing outside the door asking about this person. Something about it just kind of made me feel insecure. And you know I had an accent, so a small crowd gathered listening to my Texas twang. People wanted to talk a little bit more. And I loved it. The main woman in the office was the financial person, and she came and called me into her office via the front door. I said, "I have to talk to the supervisor about my background." I felt like I needed to be open with these people, and I said, "You need to know that I have to talk to the FBI once a week." That stopped the conversation for a second. I said, "I think they're just making sure I'm OK." After a short discussion, they said they would tell their boss and asked me to return the next day.

Mimi told me she met Pytka the following day, and he offered her a job. She told him she could do the phones since they needed another telephone operator. In Mimi's words, "Oh my God, I did it really well, and I made friends with many people—different heads of companies like the guy that ran a huge advertising company, Wieden+Kennedy, Dave Kennedy. I'd be on the call when Dave would call Joe from Portland regarding commercials such as 'Bo Knows' and others."

On the phone, Dave Kennedy kept asking, "Where are you from?" Mimi said Wichita Falls, and he asked, "But where did you come from?" When she got to Joe's office, Mimi told him she had been living in Terlingua. She learned that he grew up in Odessa and that he had a Native American background. Soon, she moved from answering the phones to working with Joe as an assistant.

As a result, Mimi did all the American Indian College Fund commercials for many years—even one in Paris, Texas. She booked the actors for several movies in Terlingua. She knew Latinos and non-Latinos and could speak enough Spanish to go across the river, put people on tape, and get an actual diverse situation.

Even though things had smoothed out, Mimi was still a little nervous. When the phone would ring, "I would freak out, wondering if *they* had found me." Mimi explained further, "Since I had to talk to the FBI every week, that was pretty hard to take a job and say that, but Joe understood. He was fascinated, and he could obviously see my stress. And it was a perfect job for me. I could control the telephones like nobody's business once I realized how to use them. Dave Kennedy and I became friends, and Joe liked that I was a Texan and that I liked people. When we would fly together up to a Wieden+Kennedy meeting, he introduced me as his little sister."

Pytka tried to write a screenplay about Mimi's story. She got hold of his lawyer and had it canceled. "It was absolutely crappy," she told me. He had Pablo with red hair, for instance. Despite his talent, he could not get this one right.

One way Mimi gauged Pytka's success was by counting up all the material Joe submitted to the advertising festival at Cannes, France, each year for award consideration. She said, "Joe, it's too much. You're the only person with fifty entries. (Most people had six or maybe twenty at the most.) It just looks like you're showing off." And he was like, "Oh my God . . ." Mimi continued, "I could talk to him that way. He was 6'8" with long blond hair, so everybody was terrified of him. He paid me out of his Pittsburgh office the whole time I worked for him to protect me. It gave me a great sense of peace that I could live places without people finding me."

In Venice, Mimi was settled. She could walk to work. The office routed her phone calls so she could not be located. When her dad came to see her, bringing some plants, Joe walked out to meet him. Her dad darted around the corner and said, "Oh my God, he looks just like

Robert." Mimi said, "He's not Robert." He was the most prominent commercial director in the world. He had a couple of Ferraris. Her dad was impressed.

In April 1991, Mimi got a message from her Texas friend Ann Richards calling to tell her that her uncle John Tower and his daughter, Marian—Mimi's cousin, whom they affectionately called "Poo"—had been killed in a commercial commuter airlines crash near St. Simon's Island, in Georgia. Mimi went to Dallas for the funeral. She and her aunt were very close.

When she arrived in Dallas, Mimi pitched in to deal with the visitors. She remembers telling George W. Bush, "Just put your wife in the kitchen and help me deal with the door." George could not stop crying. He'd answer the door and start sobbing, she told me. The line outside her cousin's Highland Park home was over a block long. "We all liked each other. The death was hard on me, too. George H.W. and Barbara Bush were there, and here I was, sitting next to Strom Thurmond, whose hair I couldn't stop looking at. It was hard because we did not have the final information yet. It was rough on me because of my cousin."

Then Mimi went home to Wichita Falls. "I helped my aunt handle all the funeral stuff because she was a wreck, and I stayed with her."

Another day, Mimi told me, "I'm standing in line at a Venice Starbucks, and I was behind somebody and wondering when it will be my turn. And suddenly, I'm like, 'Oh my god'—I could smell the perfume, and I looked at all that hairspray, and she turned around, and it was Ann [Richards]. 'What are you doing in my coffee shop?' I asked. She started to tell me, but I said, 'Don't tell me: I'll tell you! You are making a commercial with the guy I work for.'" Ann was making a Doritos commercial with Mario Cuomo for the 1995 Super Bowl.

"The first casting job I had on my own was for Michael Jackson's 'Heal the World' video, directed by Joe Pytka," Mimi said. "It was easy.

That sounds terrible, but I ate so many church dinners that I can't even tell you. And then you know Michael would call, and he was hard for me to be around, knowing his reputation for pedophilia. I didn't want him around my grandchildren. I consider Meño's children and grandchildren mine. But we did years of work with Michael Jackson"—the singer, songwriter, and dancer known as "The King of Pop." Mimi told me that she did at least ten videos with Jackson. He always had a five- or six-year-old kid with him.

Later, Mimi became the go-to person for movie companies looking for real people performers in the Big Bend region and began to step out from under Joe Pytka's shadow. I asked the name of her company. "Mimi Webb Miller Casting. I started it as 'Real People Casting' while still working for Joe." Her familiarity with the people in the Big Bend paid off. Her philosophy was to take real people, not professional actors, and film them as they are in their everyday roles. Her business thrived.

As her casting business grew, Mimi began to be recognized by a wider community in and around Venice. Her support of local artists and nonprofit organizations developed Mimi's reputation as a person who could get things done.

While Mimi established herself in the competitive world of California, she continued checking the safety climate in Lajitas and Terlingua, where she felt most at home. Her ranch was no longer available to her, having been taken over by friends of the cartel, and Mexico continued to be a no-no for her. So, she decided to make a home for herself in the Ghost Town of Terlingua, building her new house from the ruins of a long-ago miner's stacked-stone building.

Innovative Mimi didn't stop with just a place to hang out. She continued her building spree in 1996, purchasing a small group of ruins in Terlingua and reconstructing them as a hotel, naming it *La Posada Milagro*. The size of the ruins dictated the dimensions of the rooms, and she stuck to historically correct materials: stacked rock, cement, and a partially caned roof supported by hundred-year-old beams. Mimi's plans originally called for nine rooms, but the owner of the Ghost Town, Bill Ivey, restricted it to only three. Why? She does not know.

In 2008, when her stepmother was dying, Mimi went back to Wichita Falls. Ruth had come to the ranch to see her once; Mimi doesn't know whether it was a lack of affection for her or a dislike of the territory. Still, she felt the need to be with Ruth in her final hours, even though her childhood was much stricter than she'd have liked. Mimi acknowledged that Ruth did help restore her after the Lake Murray incident.

"When I saw her, my sister cautioned me to be careful about what I said because she still had her hearing." Mimi talked to her for almost two hours about her life in the Big Bend.

With the loss of her stepmother, Mimi was solidifying her connections with the Big Bend area. It was seeping into her bones. For an artist who had worked in a large city to fall in love with the most undeveloped portions of the state was something of a miracle.

Mimi mused about these contradictions in her life. Her love for fine art, big cities, fine food, and fancy clothes fell by the wayside as she contemplated the varying vistas of the Big Bend: mountains to desert, streams to waterfalls, and strange animals, including rattlesnakes and mountain lions. It's not the type of environment a well-bred debutante would choose. But something about the Big Bend made it different.

CHAPTER 9

Terlingua

Mimi wrote in an email to me on Tuesday, January 30, 2023, from her Venice, California, home, "I'm closing out my place at the beach. I have thirty-six years in it and created a vast garden area. It's hard to say goodbye. My friend and co-worker, Noemi, came with me. I rented out the tiny California apartment's bottom floor to a really good friend, Vicki Halliday. We went to SMU together. Vicki produced many commercials, such as some with Michael Jackson. And we re-met through Pytka! She was working with the advertising firm BBDO back then."

Vicki told me that she hadn't talked to Joe Pytka again. He was out of town, but she expected to see him when he returned. Joe was so incredibly good to Mimi, shielding her from all the bad stuff. And she loved him for all she learned from him.

On February 6, 2006, I was in the Big Bend again, showing off my favorite part of Texas to a couple of friends I had met in Oman. We had come from Lubbock, where my friends attended the opening of an exhibition of their photographic work at Texas Tech University. I had arranged all this during my time in Oman with the State Department's Art in Embassies program. My friends, photographer and surgeon Mac Rowley and Austin attorney Frank Calhoun, came along to be cohosts and assistant tour guides.

After the exhibition opening, we all headed south, toward the Texas mountains and Big Bend National Park.

With several stops for photography along the way, we arrived in Terlingua for the evening. I wanted them to see a genuine "Ghost Town" and meet Mimi, who had promised to give them her version of far West Texas history.

As usual, Mimi did not disappoint. She talked about how the town got its name—"an Indian legend." There was this old Mexican who said the name came from a narcotic plant that only grew along the creek. The Native Americans would harvest it to make a drink called "tizlingo," which later changed into Terlingua.

She explained that near the junction of Terlingua Creek and the Rio Grande, there was a small mining settlement named Terlingua.

Others say Terlingua got its name from a local creek called "Tres Lenguas," or "Three Tongues," in Spanish. Three Native American tribes, Apache, Comanche, and Shawnee, lived in the area, giving a clue as to the origin of the name.

A more colorful explanation comes via the story of a man studying for the priesthood who read an old Spanish document dealing with the Rio Bravo area. It told of Terlingua Creek, and a Native American village along the creek spelled the same as the town's name.

By the time quicksilver mining had gotten underway during the early twentieth century, Terlingua had thrived with upwards of 2,000 inhabitants. In the 1940s, production leveled off.

Most readers will know Terlingua as a popular chili cook-off destination, but to Mimi, it is now home.

Wrapping up the trip, my friends and I went to the bunkhouse for breakfast, enjoying eggs and bacon. There, we met Jennifer Cooper, a population biologist working on javelinas. She took us to one of their pens, where she would trap javelinas and take small tissue samples from the ears to check the DNA.

In a recent interview, Mimi told me she could not return to her home on the ranch in Mexico because it had been stolen and put in the names of a wealthy relative of Meño. I asked if she had papers showing her rights to the property. Mimi replied, "We have the paperwork, but they have done everything crooked. Someone has taken over the whole ranch. They've been stealing water for thirty-eight years. And they have a lot of money. Calderoni lived next door to Meño's cousin who stole the ranch in the country club area of Juárez. Calderoni, head of the federal police, was responsible for Pablo's death." Mimi had retained an attorney in hopes of getting the money she paid for the ranch returned.

When Mimi came back from California to live full time in the Big Bend, tourism had increased exponentially. Familiar people had moved or passed on, but many old friends remained. And Mimi hit the ground running, never missing a beat. She was able to open the hotel, coffee shop, and taqueria.

The success of Mimi's hotel, *La Posada Milagro*, encouraged her to build more rooms and add *Espressso y Poco Mas*, a coffee shop, along with a taqueria for visitors and locals. As a result, she became more

Mimi in Front of Hotel Construction Site. *Photograph by Bill Wright.*

La Posada Milagro. *Photograph by Bill Wright.*

La Posada Milagro Door. *Photograph by Bill Wright.*

La Posada Milagro Patio. *Photograph by Bill Wright.*

involved with the community, quickly renewing the camaraderie with old friends and making new ones.

Continuing the saga of regaining ownership of her ranch in Mexico, Rancho El Milagro, she told me more about her efforts to get legal help.

"The ranch has been taken away, and they're M******F******, and I'm dealing with it. And they've redone it, knocked everything down, moved the road, selling the water. They tore down the swimming pool and put in a lake. You know it's rich people from Juárez. All with no rights to be doing this. Everyone in San Carlos knows that.

"I have a specialist from Del Rio that's been here once, but coming back, who settles problems along the frontier between Mexicans and gringos that buy property on either side. I talked to the two guys. 'You know you worked for me and are watching this all go on,' so we'll see."

"So, you're filing a lawsuit against them?" I asked.

Mimi replied, "I don't exactly know what we have to do. You can do only certain things across the country right there on the border area."

"Could you at least get your money back that you paid for it?" I inquired.

"For me to take over the ranch again? It's an enormous amount for me right now. I am looking into getting a lawyer recommended by a friend. The man is the biggest tile manufacturer in North America. Everyone knows what they are doing. Very unpopular."

CHAPTER 10

Mimi, Now

On a more recent visit to see Mimi, my son Mitch joined me at the end of an interview. He sat beside her, sloshing the remnants of a Coke in his cup. Mitch had met Mimi once before when we passed through Terlingua and was familiar with her particular brand of talking: jumping from subject to subject.

"Oh my God, it's so good," she said. "It's the only thing I'm addicted to. I swear to God. Real Coca-Cola Coke. It's so funny, I never think about an adult being crazy about it."

She changed to another subject: "The purple house is on my property. I should take you to see this—it is one of the sweetest houses with a lot of art in it."

I asked Mimi about her plans for her businesses, and she turned thoughtful for a few minutes. From Mimi's café, we watched the lights begin to beam across the front porch toward the Starlight restaurant. She looked toward the river and Mexico. "My friend and employee, Noemi, and I are going to start up the trips again to Mexico, going toward Nuevo Lajitas because you can see the mouth of the Santa Elena Canyon. Nearly everybody has moved or died in that little village of Nueva Lajitas, which is not on the river. I'm just crazy. It's on the backside of my mountain. I have close friends there. Noemi grew up here. Jacinto (Chinto) lives there," she said.

As usual, Mimi had another story about her life in the Big Bend. As Mitch and I sipped cups of coffee, she told us the story of a boy who was twelve years old working for Bill Ivey when she went to work at the Trading Post. The kid arrived at 6:30 every morning and got home at 12:30 a.m. He slept across from the Trading Post. Rex Ivey, Bill Ivey's father and owner of the Ghost Town at the time, was really mean to him, and he fled. When Chinto got to the river, ready to take the boat across, a bunch of drug dealers made him move everything of his off. The Border Patrol filmed the group. Along with the drug bunch, Chinto spent many

Mimi with Her Dog. *Photograph by Bill Wright.*

years in jail. Now, he's doing well. Mimi and Chinto are close, and they work together, sprucing up the little village in Mexico, Nuevo Lajitas. Mimi hopes to get some help from the government for this project.

Mimi clarified where she's living now. "I live in the Ghost Town now owned by Bill Ivey's sons, because when you say Terlingua, you often mean the surrounding area of the Ghost Town."

After Covid restrictions lifted, I felt like traveling again and made a trip to my house in Fort Davis and a visit to Terlingua and the national park for the first time in a year, having spent the height of the pandemic in virtual isolation at my home in Abilene. My wonderful wife of sixty-three years had passed away before the pandemic hit, so I had not been to the locations where I loved to photograph and hike. Of course, I checked on Mimi. I was glad to see her back where she belongs—in her beloved Big Bend of Texas.

I found Mimi just where I thought she would be: full of plans for the future. Mimi had written me that she had taken on a script for a movie about Marfa. She was also dealing with three businesses in Ghost Town—which is part of Terlingua—unless she's in El Paso for a doctor's appointment. Noemi accompanies her for those. Even with Alzheimer's disease, Mimi packs a lot into a week. She noted that she finally had a good lawyer to help retrieve her stolen ranch. And she's realistic about the conditions in her part of Texas and all along the Rio Grande River. In a 2025 interview, Mimi told me that "they practically throw fentanyl (across the river) to you." It's that bad. And it is part of the story of the contemporary West.

Creative. Industrious. Kind. And warm. I am grateful for the opportunity to know this truly genuine person: a free spirit with a heart as big as Texas.

Bill and Mimi in 2025. *Photograph by Alison Peeler.*

TIMELINE

1926	April 17, Mimi's mother, Marian Bullington, is born.
1930s	Walter Egbert Webb (1896–1962) helps with FDR's Great Plains Shelterbelt program.
1943	Mimi's dad graduates from Wichita Falls High School.
1944	Mimi's dad enlists in service.
1946	June 1, Mimi's parents marry.
1949	April 2, Mimi is born in Wichita Falls, Texas.
1954	Mimi's mother dies.
1955	Mimi's father marries Ruth Sherrill.
1968	August, Mimi marries Alan Sullivan, who worked for IBM.
1971	December, Mimi graduates from SMU with a BFA in Ceramics and Art History.
1972	Mimi marries Dick Miller, Houston used car salesman she met in Dallas at a Greenville Avenue bar. Dick worked for a VW dealership.
	At Rice, Mimi manages the Rice Art Gallery in Sewall Hall for two and a half years.
1976	Mimi makes first trip to the Big Bend with Ann Richards.
	Six months later, at Christmas—came to Big Bend with canoe on top of Checker cab.
	Meets Mike O'Connor who dated local attorney, Liz Rogers.
	Driving back and forth to Houston—12 hours.
	Meets Pablo Acosta the day after she arrived with Robert Chambers at the cemetery in Ojinaga. Pablo handed her two joints through the car window.
1977	Moves to Lajitas as an art consultant to Walter Mischer to help found the Lajitas Museum and Foundation. Works for him two years.
	Bill Ivey hires Mimi and provides her a place at the Trading Post until she got a trailer to live in.

1978	Mimi begins guiding and outfitting horseback trips in Northern Mexico.
1979	Year residency at the Lajitas Trading Post.
1980	Meets Meño, falls in love, begins common law marriage, and helps care for his two children.[a] He had too many girlfriends, so they did not stay together.
	The Goat Incident in Houston.
1981	Purchases the 3,500-acre ranch with 40-foot waterfall.
	Not long after moving to the ranch, Mimi steps on a four-inch nail. Has ten operations on her leg. Has Mycobacterium (skeletal) tuberculosis. First case in the US. At hospital over three months.
1982	January, Bill Wright meets Mimi on trip to San Carlos. Along on the trip were Alice Wright, Philip and Jo Schultz from Santa Fe, Nancy Scanlan from Austin, Marni Sandweiss from Fort Worth, and her assistant, Charlotte Card.[b]
1986	Mimi serves as guide to adventurous American tourists on horseback trips into the Mexican mountains from her ranch: Rancho El Milagro (Miracle Ranch).
	Pablo grants an interview lasting thirteen hours with Terrence Poppa.[c] It lasts three days.
	Mimi pregnant but loses child when a neighbor in Mexico fires at her during a disagreement over his goat-grazing practices. Her horse was spooked when she tried to get off and it bucked her, and she miscarried that night alone.[d]
1986, 1987	Mimi and Acosta see each other for less than a year before he is killed in the shootout with authorities.[e]
1987	April 22, one of Acosta's nephews picks Mimi up after she returned some tourists to Lajitas. He takes her to Santa Elena, Pablo's birthplace, to say goodbye.[f]
	April 24, Pablo Acosta is killed.
	Mimi joins a scientific study on depression in Fort Worth.[g]
	A bounty is set on Mimi's life, and she spends almost three years on the run.
	Moves to Los Angeles to begin working the phones for Joe Pytka. Later becomes his assistant.
	Finds work as a casting director in Los Angeles.[h]

1989	January 20, Mimi receives a letter from Curtis Tunnell, ED of the Texas Historical Commission, thanking her for visiting in November, enclosing photos of Pablo's grave, and inviting her to come back to Austin for an oral history interview.
	June 6, Mimi sends Bill a note attached to her concept paper for a feature film based on a true story "Borderline: The Gringa and the Mafioso." Co-writer is Sherry Abaldo.
1994	Becomes casting director of own company: Mimi Webb Miller Casting.[i]
1997	Returns from California to live part time in the Big Bend. Rancho El Milagro Horseback/Adventure Trips Chihuahua, Mexico.
2005	Opens La Posada Milagro Guesthouse.
	Opens Espresso y Poco Mas.
2006	February 8, Bill Wright arrives in Terlingua and sees Mimi and her new hotel. Ate together in Study Bute with Mimi and a friend and then went on to Santa Elena Canyon.
2018	Mimi portrayed by Sosie Bacon in four episodes of the second season of *Narcos: Mexico*, a Netflix television series exploring the 1980s roots of Mexican drug trafficking. Depicts Mimi's association (as girlfriend) with "The Ojinaga Fox," drug kingpin Pablo Acosta Villarreal.
Then and Today	Suffers from PTSD that left her struggling to make sense of those years, especially her time with Acosta.[j]

Timeline sources:

[a] Stephen Paulsen, "Terlingua woman portrayed on Narcos: Mexico recalls life with 'The Ojinaga Fox,'" *The Big Bend Sentinel*, May 13, 2020.

[b] See Bill Wright, *Portraits from the Desert: Bill Wright's Big Bend* (University of Texas Press, 1998), 37.

[c] Larry Birnbaum and Will Delgadillo, "Pablo Acosta: The Fox of Ojinaga," *Spin Magazine*, June 1990.

[d] Paulson, "Terlingua woman portrayed on Narcos."

[e] Paulson, "Terlingua woman portrayed on Narcos."

[f] Birnbaum and Delgadillo, "The Fox of Ojinaga."

[g] Paulson, "Terlingua woman portrayed on Narcos."

[h] Paulson, "Terlingua woman portrayed on Narcos."

[i] Leatherwood, *Why Terlingua*, ch.5, n.3

[j] Paulson, "Terlingua woman portrayed on Narcos."

POSTSCRIPT BY MIMI WEBB MILLER

I am grateful for the release of this book.

It was created over a period of three years while I was moving from California back to my beloved Texas. My good friend, Bill Wright, who assembled my recollections with the help of his assistant, Marianne Wood, was often frustrated but never relented in pursuit of my life's story. I hope you enjoy it. It's as accurate as I can remember.

Mimi Webb Miller

Mimi Webb Miller

ACKNOWLEDGMENTS

Unless you are living under a rock, knowledge of drug smuggling and the devastating hardships that this trade inflicts on every person in its wake disturbs you greatly. Human smuggling networks parallel the drug ones. Cartels work both aspects. Just Google it. Or read a marvelous new book from TCU Press by Sergio Chapa and Guadalupe Correa-Cabrera called *Frontera: A Journey across the US-Mexico Border.* With helpful maps and photographic illustrations, the authors give readers a good examination of this beautiful yet complex part of the world. A world that Mimi loves. I do, too.

I wish to thank David Regela for allowing me to interview him and to quote from his wonderful book, *Against the Wind.* James C. Marchant's *Distrito Bravo: The Outlaw District* also helped me tell Mimi's story. And my interview with Terrence E. Poppa, author of *Drug Lord: The Life and Death of a Mexican Kingpin*, provided essential information. Each person's work bolsters the mandate that we must work together to eradicate the dangers associated with the drug trade. We must make the land welcome to visitors and residents alike.

In addition, I wish to thank the following: Bill Ivey, Liz Rogers, John Bintliff, Judy Vetter, and James Surls. Each generously gave me their takes on this kind, colorful, and talented woman of the Far West.

I especially want to thank Melissa and Jim Hogan, Mimi's sister and brother-in-law, who granted me an interview in their home. They provided a fresh insight into Mimi's intricate life.

I also thank Carol Rudd, an archivist at the Wichita County Archives, for her cheerful and generous service to me as I searched for the nitty gritty details that would bring Mimi's story to life.

Van Robinson, a friend and voracious reader in Fort Davis, read and enthusiastically commented on an early draft. So did Glenn Dromgoole, retired *Abilene Reporter-News* editor, who offered valuable suggestions using his immense expertise.

Jennifer Morehead, multiplatform editor at *The Washington Post* and family friend, gave me expert recommendations for tidying my manuscript and making it clearer.

And without the help of my editorial assistant and researcher, Marianne Wood, this book would not be in your hands today.

Above all, I thank Mimi Webb Miller and her family for allowing me to tell her amazing story!

NOTES

CHAPTER 2. GETTING STARTED: MIMI'S EARLY YEARS

1. "Farming in the US," *American Experience: PBS,* last accessed September 10, 2025, https://www.pbs.org/wgbh/americanexperience/features/troublesome-farming-us/.
2. "Farming in the US," *American Experience: PBS.*

CHAPTER 3. COLLEGE AND FIRST MARRIAGE

1. Elena Nicolaou, "Mimi Webb Miller of *Narcos: Mexico* Opens up About Her Last Day with Pablo Acosta," *Oprah Daily,* February 19, 2020, last accessed September 10, 2025, https://oprahdaily.com/entertainment/tv-movies/a30765909/mimi-webb-miller-narcos-now/.

CHAPTER 5: BIG BEND CALLING

1. Blair Pittman, *Tales From the Terlingua Porch* (Sun Country Publications, 2009), 53.
2. Terrence E. Poppa, *Drug Lord: The Life and Death of a Mexican Kingpin* (Demand Publications, 1998), 228.
3. Carlton Leatherwood, *Why Terlingua: Adventure on the Edge of Texas* (Menagerie Press, 2009), 40.
4. Jefferson Morgenthaler, *The River Has Never Divided Us: A Border History of La Junta de los Rios* (University of Texas Press, 2004), 216.

CHAPTER 6: PABLO

1. Terrence E. Poppa, *Drug Lord: The Life and Death of a Mexican Kingpin* (Demand Publications, 1998), 219–21.
2. David Regela, *Against the Wind: Fighting America's Drug War on the Rio Grande* (Regson Publishing, 2022), 143.
3. Poppa, *Drug Lord,* 222.
4. Poppa, *Drug Lord,* 259.
5. Poppa, *Drug Lord,* 260–61.
6. Walt Harrigan, "The Last Days of the Lawless West: What the guerilla kidnapping of Refugio Gonzalez really means," *Washington Post,* April 6, 1986.
7. Harrigan, "The Last Days of the Lawless West."
8. Poppa, *Drug Lord,* 259.
9. Poppa, *Drug Lord,* 259.
10. Poppa, *Drug Lord,* 262.
11. Regela, *Against the Wind,* 219.

12. Bill Wright Interview with Boyd Chambers, *The Texas Outback: Ranching on the Last Frontier* (Texas A&M University Press, 2005), 28.
13. David Regela, *Against the Wind: Fighting America's Drug War on the Rio Grande* (Regson Publishing, 2022), 207.
14. Terrence E. Poppa, "Pablo Acosta: He says he is a minor drug smuggler with a desire to help others. But officials charge he is a key player in the border drug trade, a Mexican Godfather," *El Paso Herald-Post*, December 3, 1986.
15. Poppa, *Drug Lord,* 293. For more information and photos, please visit the following links: https://www.pbs.org/wgbh/pages/frontline/shows/drugs/interviews/calderoni.html, https://druglord.com/cast-of-characters/pablo-acosta/.
16. James C. Marchant, *Distrito Bravo: The Outlaw District* (published by the author, 2022), 292.
17. Regela, *Against the Wind*, 224.
18. Elena Nicolaou, "Mimi Webb Miller of *Narcos: Mexico* Opens up About Her Last Day with Pablo Acosta," *Oprah Daily*, February 19, 2020, https://oprahdaily.com/entertainment/tv-movies/a30765909/mimi-webb-miller-narcos-now/.

CHAPTER 7: EL PASO

1. David Regela, *Against the Wind: Fighting America's Drug War on the Rio Grande* (Regson Publishing, 2022), 237.

ABOUT THE AUTHOR

Accomplished businessman, author, and photographer Bill Wright has explored and recorded journeys from all over the globe. Never letting the grass grow under his feet for long, his fourteenth book, *Mimi: The Perilous Journey of a Free-Spirited Texas Woman*, was published the year he turned ninety-three!

Bill splits his time between homes in Abilene and Fort Davis and enjoys the companionship of family and friends, including a rescued goldendoodle named Brie.

www.ingramcontent.com/pod-product-compliance
Lightning Source LLC
Chambersburg PA
CBHW030049180326
41440CB00022B/543
9780875659633